What Works
in Girls' Education

Evidence and Policies from the Developing World

BARBARA HERZ *and* GENE B. SPERLING

COUNCIL ON
FOREIGN
RELATIONS

Contents

Foreword

Over the last several years, it has become increasingly clear that quality universal basic education in poor countries is not only critical to economic progress and global poverty reduction but also has important implications for broader foreign policy goals.

That is why in 2002 the Council on Foreign Relations started the Center for Universal Education with Senior Fellow Gene B. Sperling as its director.

While we continue to struggle to understand many foreign policy and development challenges, the issue of girls' education is unique: a striking body of empirical evidence demonstrates its strong benefits across a broad range of areas, from children's health and broader educational attainment, to social stability and economic growth. Even in countries where the social and cultural obstacles to educating or empowering girls may seem overwhelming, a strategic mix of proven policies and programs can ensure girls are in school and make a critical difference to their and their societies' long-term success.

This report brings together the best scholarly analyses on this topic and organizes their findings into an easy-to-use guide for policymakers and their staffs. It was written by Barbara Herz, who brings more than 20 years of expertise in girls' education at the U.S. Agency for International Development, the World Bank, and the U.S. Treasury, and Gene B. Sperling, who represented the United States at the 2000 World Education Forum in Dakar, Senegal.

The Council would like to thank the William and Flora Hewlett Foundation and the Carnegie Corporation for their financial support of this project.

Richard N. Haass
President
Council on Foreign Relations

Acknowledgments

We began this project to bring together the vast literature on the benefits of girls' education into a single, user-friendly reference guide for policymakers and opinion leaders. We cast a wide net and tried to identify the best and most relevant studies and findings. Through this process, we have been extremely fortunate to have some of the top experts in the world review this report and offer suggestions, advice, and critiques. In our effort to be concise and accessible, we recognize that we cannot capture the complexity and depth of all the research, and all omissions and errors are the sole responsibility of the authors.

We thank the following people for reviewing the paper and sharing their comments throughout this process: Barbara Bruns and Carolyn Winter at the World Bank; Cream Wright, Education Chief at UNICEF; Christopher Colclough, coordinator of the 2003/4 EFA Global Monitoring Report at UNESCO; Nancy Birdsall and Ruth Levine at the Center for Global Development; George Ingram at the Basic Education Coalition; Patrick Watt at ActionAid in the United Kingdom; Lawrence Chickering; Andrea Rugh; Oliver Buston; and Caren Grown at the International Center for Research on Women. For providing extensive materials, special thanks go to Elizabeth King of the World Bank. For their assistance with our discussion of HIV/AIDS, we also would like to thank Don Bundy, Brad Strickland, Alexandra Draxler, and Tania Boler. For their guidance on overall issues pertaining to Africa, we would like to thank Gayle Smith, Susan Rice, Catherine Byrne, and Princeton Lyman. We also would like to thank people whose work and advice in this area has inspired us and given us direction: Carol Bellamy at UNICEF; Lawrence H. Summers at Harvard University; Ruth Kagia at the World

Bank; Paul Schultz at Yale University; Steven Moseley at the Academy for Educational Development; D. Joseph Wood, Ann Hamilton, and Paul Isenman, formerly of the World Bank; Richard Samans at the World Economic Forum; Geeta Rao Gupta at the International Center for Research on Women; Amina Ibrahim, National Coordinator for Education for All at the Federal Ministry of Education in Nigeria; Ann-Therese Ndong-Jatta, Secretary of State for Education from the Gambia; and Ashfaq Mahmood, former Secretary, Planning, of Pakistan.

We would like to thank our colleagues at the Council on Foreign Relations, including Leslie H. Gelb, Michael P. Peters, and Lee Feinstein for their support in undertaking this project, and James M. Lindsay and Richard N. Haass for seeing it through to completion. We also would like to thank Marshall Smith and Tamara Fox at the William and Flora Hewlett Foundation for their support and guidance, and Susan King at the Carnegie Corporation for her strategic suggestions and comments.

This report would not have been possible without the dedication and excellent assistance of various research staff. We would like especially to thank Rekha Balu, Brian Deese, Oeindrila Dube, and John Neffinger. We also benefited from the assistance of two college interns, Sara Aronchick and Cate Edwards.

Finally, we thank the Council on Foreign Relations for hosting the Center for Universal Education and supporting this project. We wish to thank the William and Flora Hewlett Foundation for their overall support for the Center for Universal Education, and we would like to thank the Carnegie Corporation for underwriting the publication and distribution of this report.

Barbara Herz
Gene B. Sperling

Executive Summary

The persistent problem of the tens of millions of children across the developing world who grow up without receiving the most basic education has attracted increased public attention in recent years. This crisis is acute in rural and poor areas of sub-Saharan Africa, the Middle East, and South Asia. More than 180 governments have committed to addressing this crisis by pledging that every boy and girl will receive a quality basic education by 2015. This target is now firmly established and endorsed as one of the eight United Nations Millennium Development Goals.

Yet to reach the overall goal of universal education for children, policymakers will need to make special efforts to address the economic, social, and cultural barriers that keep even larger proportions of girls in poor countries out of school. Indeed, extensive research confirms that investing in girls' education delivers high returns not only for female educational attainment, but also for maternal and children's health, more sustainable families, women's empowerment, democracy, income growth, and productivity.

This paper summarizes the extensive body of research on the state of girls' education in the developing world today; the impact of educating girls on families, economies, and nations; and the most promising approaches to increasing girls' enrollment and educational quality. The overall conclusions are straightforward: educating girls pays off *substantially*. While challenges still exist, existing research provides us guidance on how to make significant progress.

I. The State of Girls' Education

- **104 million children aged 6–11 are not in school each year—60 million are girls.** Nearly 40 percent of these out-of-school children live in sub-Saharan Africa; 35 percent live in South Asia (UNESCO 2003a).

- **Studies find that 150 million children currently enrolled in school will drop out before completing primary school—at least 100 million are girls** (World Bank 2002a).

  - Only 36 of the 155 developing countries have achieved 100 percent primary school completion rates (World Bank 2002a).

  - Across the developing world, the gender gap between boys and girls in primary school completion is greater than 10 percentage points. UNICEF emphasizes that "this yawning gender gap means that millions more girls than boys are dropping out each year" (UNICEF 2003).

- **In sub-Saharan Africa, more than half of girls—54 percent—do not complete even a primary school education** (Bruns et al. 2003).

  - In Chad, 90 percent of all 15- to 19-year-old girls had not completed even primary school, and in Burkina Faso, 80 percent had not done so, according to a 1999 study (Filmer 1999).

- **In South Asia, more than 40 percent of girls aged 15–19 from poor households never completed first grade;** only one in four completed fifth grade (Filmer and Pritchett 1999).

- **After primary school, girls' participation plummets further—only 17 percent of girls in Africa are enrolled in secondary school** (UNESCO 2003a).

  - In Cambodia, only 12 percent of girls enroll in secondary school, and in Laos, fewer than one in four girls attend beyond the primary level (UNESCO 2003b).

- **The difference between urban and rural areas is striking, especially for girls.**

  - In Niger, 83 percent of girls in the capital of Niamey are enrolled in primary school, compared to 12 percent in rural areas (World Bank 1996b).

  - In Pakistan, the primary school completion rate for boys in rural areas is three times higher than for girls; in urban areas it is twice as high (World Bank 1996a).

- **At least one in three girls completing primary school in Africa and South Asia cannot effectively read, write, or do simple arithmetic.**

  - In Egypt, reading and writing scores on national exams are about half of mastery level. In Pakistan, pass rates on national exams at the end of primary school have been set at 30 percent because few children are expected to do better (Fredriksen 2002a, World Bank 1996a).

II. The Benefits of Girls' Education

A. Education and Income Growth: Girls' education leads to increased income, both for individuals and for nations as a whole. While educating both boys and girls increases productivity and supports the growth of national economies, the education of girls may lead to greater income gains.

1. Higher Wages

   - **Providing girls one extra year of education beyond the average boosts eventual wages by 10–20 percent.** Studies have found returns to primary education on the order of 5 to 15 percent for boys and slightly higher for girls. A recent study concludes, "Overall, women receive higher returns to their schooling investments" (Psacharopoulos and Patrinos 2002).

   - **A leading development economist has found that returns to female secondary education are in the 15–25 percent range.** Yale economist Paul Schultz has found that wage gains from additional education tend to be similar if not somewhat higher for women than for men, and that the returns to secondary education in particular are generally appreciably higher for women (Schultz 2002).

2. Faster Economic Growth

   - **A 100-country study by the World Bank shows that increasing the share of women with a secondary education by 1 percent boosts annual per capita income growth by 0.3 percentage points.** This is a substantial amount considering that per capita income gains in developing countries seldom exceed 3 percent a year (Dollar and Gatti 1999).

   - **More equal education levels between men and women could have led to nearly 1 percent higher annual per capita growth in gross domestic product (GDP) in South Asia and sub-Saharan Africa during 1960–92** (Klasen 1999).

3. More Productive Farming

   - **More productive farming due to increased female education accounts for 43 percent of the decline in malnutrition achieved between 1970 and 1995,** according to a 63-country study (Smith and Haddad 1999).

   - **If women farmers in Kenya had the same education and inputs as men farmers, crop yields could rise 22 percent** (Quisumbing 1996).

B. Education and Smaller, Healthier, Better-Educated Families: A wealth of cross-country and individual country studies from Africa, Asia, and Latin America reveals a pattern: women with more education have smaller, healthier, and better-educated families. As education expands women's horizons, opens up better earning opportunities, and improves women's position in the family and society, couples tend to have fewer children and to invest more in the health and education of each child.

1. **Educating Girls Leads to Smaller, More Sustainable Families**

    - **When women gain four years more education, fertility per woman drops by roughly one birth,** according to a 100-country World Bank study (Klasen 1999).

    - **A 65-country analysis finds that doubling the proportion of women with a secondary education would reduce average fertility rates from 5.3 to 3.9 children per woman.** The authors conclude,

        ◆ "The expansion of female secondary education may be the best single policy for achieving substantial reductions in fertility" (Subbarao and Raney 1995).

    - **A study of Brazil finds that illiterate women have an average of 6 children each, while literate women have an average of 2.5 children each** (UNESCO 2000).

2. **Educating Women Saves Children's Lives**

    - **An extra year of girls' education can reduce infant mortality by 5–10 percent.** This link "is especially striking in low income countries. The pattern has been widely replicated across comparative data bases . . . and through repeated censuses" (Schultz 1993).

    - **In Africa, children of mothers who receive five years of primary education are 40 percent more likely to live beyond age five** (Summers 1994).

    - **Multicountry data show educated mothers are about 50 percent more likely to immunize their children than uneducated mothers are** (Gage et al. 1997).

3. **Educating Women Promotes Educating Children**

    - **A recent cross-country study finds that women's education generally has more impact than men's education on children's schooling** (Filmer 2000).

    - **An Indian study finds that children of educated women study two extra hours per day** (Behrman et al. 1999).

C. Education and HIV/AIDS: In the 1980s, early in the AIDS pandemic, HIV infection rates tended to be higher among more-educated people, which researchers attribute to the timing of the epidemic and the increased mobility of better-educated people. In the 1990s, however, things changed. Now an increasing body of research shows that more-educated people, especially youth, are less likely to engage in risky behavior and contract HIV.

1. **Educated Girls Are Less Likely to Contract HIV**

    - **A 72-country analysis finds that where the literacy gap between boys and girls exceeds 25 percent, HIV prevalence exceeds 5 percent—the cited outbreak level.** Conversely, HIV prevalence falls below 3 percent where the literacy gap is below 5 percent (Over 1998).

    - **A study of Zambia finds that AIDS spreads twice as fast among uneducated girls** (Vandemoortele and Delamonica 2000).

    - **Young rural Ugandans with secondary education are three times less likely than those with no education to be HIV positive** (De Walque 2004).

    - **A Kenyan study finds that girls who stay in school are four times more likely to be virgins than those who drop out** (UNICEF 2002b).

2. **School-Based Education Programs Help Prevent HIV Infection**

    - **A Ugandan program reduced by 75 percent the number of sexually active children in their last year of primary school** (Shuey et al. 1999).

    - **A review of 113 studies indicates that school-based AIDS education programs are effective in reducing early sexual activity and high-risk behavior** (Kirby et al. 1994).

D. Education and Empowered Women: Increased female education is one of the most powerful tools to empower women within the family and society. As that happens, women not only improve their own welfare but, through their "agency," act to improve the well-being of their children and help transform society itself (A. Sen 2000). This empowerment of women comes from greater years of education—but it also comes as women catch up with men in education even when average levels of education remain quite low. Nobel laureate Amartya Sen argues that "the changing agency of women is one of the major mediators of economic and social change. . . . Nothing, arguably, is as important today in the political economy of development as adequate recognition of political, economic, and social participation and leadership of women."

1. **Education Can Reduce Domestic Violence**

   - **Research on India finds less violence against women where women are more educated.** Women with no formal schooling are less likely to resist violence than women with some schooling (P. Sen 1999).

2. **Education Can Decrease the Risk of Genital Mutilation**

   - **Several studies find that in Africa female genital mutilation is more prevalent among less-educated women.** The report concludes, "Those [women] with primary or no education are more likely to have been cut than those who have received secondary level instruction" (Population Reference Bureau 2001).

   - **Educated women in Burkina Faso are 40 percent less likely to subject their daughters to the practice** (World Health Organization 1998).

3. **Educated Women Spend a Greater Proportion of Their Resources on the Health and Education of Their Families**

   - **In Brazil, women's resources have 20 times the impact on children's health compared with men's resources** (Thomas 1990).

4. **Education Can Foster Democracy and Women's Political Participation**

   - **A 100-country study finds educating girls and reducing the gender gap tends to promote democracy.** The study argues that these findings confirm the hypothesis that "expanded educational opportunities for females goes along with a social structure that is generally more participatory and, hence, more receptive to democracy" (Barro 1999).

   - **Educated Bangladeshi women are three times as likely as illiterate women to participate in political meetings** (UNESCO 2000).

III. Understanding the Disconnect

The Benefits of Girls' Education versus the Low Levels of Girls' Enrollment and Attainment

If education benefits girls, their families, and society, why do we not see more girls being educated for longer periods of time?

- **Education is the quintessential public good.** If education is not made effectively mandatory, the decision to educate children falls to the parents, who incur costs now and who cannot capture much of the benefits, since they accrue across a child's lifetime and to society as a whole. Therefore, a determination based solely on the cost-benefit calculation of parents may lead to a nation's underinvesting in education.

- **Governments in developing countries need to implement policies that align the cost-benefit calculations of parents with the costs and benefits to their nations as a whole.** The most effective way for governments to do so is to make universal education (primary as step one, but also secondary) free and mandatory, while undertaking reforms to improve the quality and benefits of education. Achieving quality universal education may require substantial national and external resources and may, for a number of countries, be beyond immediate reach.

To educate girls, the need for government intervention is even greater, because the costs may seem higher to parents and the benefits more distant and harder to capture.

- **Less clear and more distant benefits:** Where daughters traditionally "marry out" of their families and join their husbands', parents may doubt how much they will benefit from having more-educated daughters.

- **Four costs to parents of educating girls:**

  1. **Direct fees:** Studies show fees for tuition can amount to 5–10 percent of household income—or 20–30 percent in poorer families. The fees may be similar for girls and boys, but parents may be less willing to pay them for girls.

  2. **Indirect fees:** Parents are sometimes charged fees for things like parent-teacher associations or to supplement teacher salaries. These fees can sometimes be as much as the cost of tuition.

  3. **Indirect costs:** Parents sometimes also face a number of indirect costs associated with sending children to school, such as for transportation, clothing, and safety. These costs may be greater for girls than for boys because of the need to ensure modesty or meet cultural requirements, such as the cost of escorts for girls.

4. The **opportunity cost** of having girls in school, in terms of lost chore time and contributions to family income, is a formidable barrier as well. In many African and Asian countries, daughters are the victims of a self-fulfilling prophecy: as they are traditionally expected to do more chores at home than are sons, the opportunity cost of educating them seems higher and so they are kept home.

IV. What Works to Educate Girls

The Evidence

Effective government intervention to get girls in school must offset the increased costs for parents of sending their girls to school and improve school quality to enhance the benefit side of the equation for both parents and the country as a whole. Most evidence suggests that what is needed is a package of policies and programs in four areas to improve girls' access to and achievement in education.

A. Make Girls' Schooling Affordable: The fastest and most direct way for governments to boost school enrollments is to reduce the direct, indirect, and opportunity costs to parents of educating their daughters.

1. Reduce Direct Costs: Cutting School Fees Increases Girls' Enrollment

   - **Enrollment in Uganda jumped 70 percent after fees were cut as part of major school reforms.** In Uganda, total girls' enrollments went from 63 percent to 83 percent, while enrollment among the poorest fifth of girls went from 46 percent to 82 percent (Bruns et al. 2003, Deininger 2003).

   - **Attendance doubled in Tanzania after eliminating fees** (Bruns et al. 2003).

   - **Asian countries including China, Korea, and Sri Lanka also boosted enrollments by reducing fees** (Herz et al. 1991).

2. Cover Indirect Costs and Compensate for Opportunity Costs: Scholarships, Stipends, and School Health and Nutrition Programs

   - **The pilot areas in Bangladesh's Female Secondary School Stipend Program saw girls' enrollment rise to double the national average.** The stipend covers tuition, books, uniforms, and transportation (World Bank 2001b). The program has been extended nationwide, and now 55–60 percent of girls and boys are enrolled in secondary school (Khandkher and Pitt 2003).

   - **The Mexican PROGRESA Program helps those who enroll in primary school complete the cycle.** The program gives poor families cash awards to cover the opportunity cost of sending kids to school, a feature that has especially helped girls. It has become a model for other such scholarship programs across Latin America (Schultz 2004, Morley and Coady 2003).

   - **Brazil's Bolsa Escola stipend program virtually eliminated dropouts.** Preliminary evaluations suggest it will help enroll one-third of all out-of-school children aged 10–15 (Lavinas 2001, Morley and Coady 2003).

B. Build Local Schools with Community Support and Flexible Schedules: An extensive body of research shows that building decent schools with adequate supplies and teachers nearby boosts girls' enrollment by making school a practical option and encouraging parents to get more involved in the education of their children.

1. **Building Schools Close to Girls' Homes Boosts Enrollments**

   - **Egypt: Constructing new schools in rural areas during the 1980s boosted girls' enrollments by 60 percent.** Rural boys' enrollments increased by 19 percent (Rugh 2000).

   - **Malaysia: The absence of a secondary school in the community lowers the probability of girls' attendance by 17 percent and boys' by 13 percent** (World Bank 2001a).

2. **Community Involvement in Local Schools Is Key**

   - **Nonformal schools run by the Bangladesh Rural Action Committee (BRAC) achieved nearly double the completion rates of government schools—90 percent versus 53 percent.** The program focuses on involving communities in transitioning the hardest-to-reach populations from informal, more flexible BRAC schools into the formal system (Rugh and Bossert 1998, Herz 2002).

   - **Colombia's Escuela Nueva program of multigrade community schools contributed to a 30 percent increase in rural enrollment** (Benveniste and McEwan 2000).

   - **A study in Pakistan finds that rural community-based schools increase girls' enrollments to more than four times the provincial average** (World Bank 1996a).

3. **Providing Flexible Schedules for Safe Schools Helps Enroll Girls**

   - **A study of Bangladesh's BRAC program finds flexible "satellite" schools increase girls' primary school enrollments** (Herz 2002).

   - **In Pakistan's Northern Areas, double sessions in community schools are key to raising girls' enrollments** (Herz 2002).

4. **Providing Preschool and Child-Care Programs Appears Promising**

   - **India: Programs offering early education near or in village primary schools increase girls' enrollment** (Rugh 2000).

   - **Kenya: A 10 percent jump in child-care costs cuts girls' attendance by 13 percent** (Lokshin et al. 2000).

C. **Make Schools More Girl-Friendly:** Providing a basic school nearby, with a teacher and books, is an important first step to increasing girls' enrollment. But to both enroll and keep girls in school, in many circumstances other measures are also necessary to meet cultural and practical needs. Fortunately, many of these can be accomplished at relatively little cost:

1. **Private Latrine Facilities Are a Must**

   - **A Pakistan study finds that parents require toilet facilities for girls** (World Bank 1996a).

   - **Girls in Africa miss school during menses if no private toilet is available** (Forum for African Women Educationalists 2001).

2. **Ensuring Girls' Privacy and Safety in Line with Cultural Requirements Is Key**

   - In some cases, cultural requirements for privacy entail measures such as separate schools for girls, boundary walls for girls' schools, or separate hours for girls in schools shared with boys. **Such measures are critical not only for increasing enrollments, but also for achieving gender parity in primary education** (World Bank 2001a).

3. **Teach in Ways That Discourage Gender Stereotypes and Encourage Girls to Achieve**

   - **Studies find traditional curricula and materials often portray women as passive** (Gachukia et al. 1992, Obura 1985, Biraimah 1980, Ethiopian Ministry of Education 1980).

     - A study of one country's curriculum found that while males mentioned were often described as leaders, fighters, or soldiers, females were most often described as breast-feeders, fertile, pretty, or pregnant (Obura 1985).

   - **In Nigeria, studies find teaching favors boys.** Boys are given more opportunities to ask and answer questions, to use learning materials, and to lead groups; girls are given less time on task than boys in science (UNICEF 2002a).

4. **Provide Female Teachers for Girls**

   - **Experience in many countries finds that having female teachers encourages girls' enrollment.**

     - **Some cultures require female teachers especially for older girls, and female teachers can also be important role models.**

     - Countries such as Bangladesh, Pakistan, and India have set national goals for hiring women teachers recently. As a result, tens of thousands of qualified women have joined the teaching force in South Asia and Africa (World Bank 2001a, Herz 2002).

- **Studies find even very young women can teach programmed curricula effectively, if they are trained and given support.** Sometimes finding qualified women teachers is difficult, and age and education requirements may have to be temporarily eased. But this doesn't have to mean a decline in quality (Kim et al. 1998, Khandkher 1996, Rugh 2000).

D. **Focus Particularly on the Quality of Education:** Where parents are more ambivalent about educating girls, improvements in education quality may be particularly important to tip their decisions to educate daughters as well as sons. As a first step, to function effectively, any school needs enough qualified teachers who attend school regularly.

What children learn also matters. In some countries, curricula are outmoded, and some may even perpetuate gender and ethnic stereotypes or misinformation. In other cases, countries may provide a good curriculum but insufficient teacher training. Schools are more effective at attracting girls if they teach curricula that equip children for the twenty-first century, and if they have the requisite books and learning materials.

1. **Provide Enough Teachers**

   - **Countries should aim to reduce maximum class size to forty students,** research shows, and insist that teachers attend more regularly. The World Bank has determined that a 40-to-1 student-to-teacher ratio can help ensure access and quality (UNICEF 2002a, Bruns et al. 2003).

   - **Indonesian experience shows that teachers are key to the expansion of enrollment for both boys and girls** (Duflo 2001).

2. **Improve Teachers' Education and Training Levels**

   - **Studies from Kenya and Bangladesh find quality of teaching influences demand for education for girls even more than for boys** (Lloyd et al. 1998, Khandkher 1996).

   - **A Swaziland study finds teacher training helped raise girls' enrollments to boys' level** (Gilmore 1997).

3. **Provide a Curriculum That Equips Children for the Twenty-first Century, with a Focus on Math and Science**

   - **In Kenya, parents are more willing to pay to send girls to school if girls can study science** (Herz et al. 1991).

   - In Brazil, Swaziland, and Uganda, as part of broader education reforms, curricula were revamped to focus more on issues of greater relevance, to broaden beyond basics, and to encourage problem solving (Herz 2002).

4. **Provide Adequate Books and Supplies**

- **A Peru study finds providing textbooks raises girls' enrollments 30 percent.** When free textbooks were supplied to primary schools, controlling for other influences, girls were 30 percent more likely to enroll, but no effect was recorded for boys' enrollments (King and Bellew 1991).

- **A multicountry study finds that textbooks boost enrollment and achievement** (Rugh 2000).

V. Getting the Job Done

The central policy question has moved beyond *what* works to educate girls and should now focus on *how* to build support for and provide affordable, quality education. Extensive research from countries that have undertaken reforms suggests that countries can make rapid progress and reach universal education, if they successfully address three critical components:

A. **Leadership and Political Will at the Country Level:** Experience from countries such as China, Morocco, Sri Lanka, and Uganda suggests high-level government leadership is key to raising the profile of girls' education and making progress on getting more girls in school (World Bank 2002a).

- **In Uganda, with President Yoweri Museveni's leadership on extensive education reform, budget support for primary education increased from 11 percent to 22 percent.** If Uganda's education spending and increasing enrollment continue, the World Bank projects the country will achieve universal primary education by 2015 (Bruns et al. 2003).

B. **Developing Comprehensive National Education Strategies**

- **The commitment of more than 180 countries to the UN Dakar Framework of Action on achieving universal education by 2015 embodies a global compact between poor countries and donors:**

  - Poor countries agree to develop comprehensive, nationally owned strategies for achieving universal education. Such plans include a clear domestic fiscal objective and commitment to education reforms. Donors agree that where such plans are credible and accountable, and where performance shows a demonstrated ability to reform, no country should fail due to lack of resources.

  - Research suggests that developing a carefully prioritized national education strategy and regularly assessing performance can catalyze rapid and substantial improvements in girls' (and boys') education (Sperling 2001, Herz 2002).

- **The Education for All Fast Track Initiative moves donors toward a global compact.** The initiative, a financing structure organized by the World Bank, creates a coordinated process for donors to support poor countries that develop and implement comprehensive national education strategies (Sperling 2003a).

- **The World Bank has developed guidelines for national education plans within the Fast Track process based on the class sizes and fiscal targets associated with successful reforms in poor countries** (Bruns et al. 2003).

- Beyond these guidelines, the most successful national plans have incorporated strong, credible budget transparency and antifraud provisions (Sperling 2003c, Moseley 2003).

C. Mobilizing Internal and External Resources

- **A 56-country analysis established a strong relationship between adequate public spending and boosting primary school enrollments** (Fredriksen 2002b). Countries on track to achieve universal education, such as Bolivia and Uganda, spent more on primary education—1.7 percent of GDP on average, versus a 1.4 percent average across all countries studied—and maintained reasonable unit costs for facilities, supplies, and teacher salaries.

- **Currently, donor assistance for primary education in poor countries is estimated at $1.4 billion annually** (World Bank 2004, OECD 2004).

- **Yet the external resources required to achieve universal basic education are at least an additional $5–$10 billion per year,** particularly if country strategies include effective but expensive programs such as stipends to get more girls in schools and efforts to address HIV/AIDS (Sperling 2003c, UNESCO 2002a).

- **A contingent commitment of donor funds could offer a "third way" beyond the traditional resource debate, jump-starting a global compact on universal education.** By making a strong commitment of ex ante resources, but disbursing funds over time and only when recipient countries develop credible plans and demonstrate sound performance, donors' budgets are not immediately affected. Yet such a commitment empowers countries already committed to serious national reforms and provides strong incentives for countries that are not quite there (Sperling 2003a).

- **High-level political commitment from the members of the G8 group of highly industrialized countries could assure the necessary political and financial resources for the Education for All Fast Track Initiative.** The next two G8 meetings—the June 2004 meeting hosted by the United States and the 2005 meeting hosted by the United Kingdom—may provide a critically important window of opportunity for generating the kind of political and financial support necessary to turn the Fast Track Initiative's progress to date into a true global compact on universal education. Such a commitment from donor countries can be critical to the success of country plans, and to the credibility of the Education for All goal as much more than another lofty, but empty, promise.

VI. Conclusion

An overwhelming body of research demonstrates that investing in girls' education delivers high returns for economic growth and broad benefits ranging from smaller families, to disease prevention, to women's well-being. Educating girls as well as boys is an achievable goal and attainable in the near term, if substantial resources are matched with comprehensive nationally owned plans for education reform that include measures of accountability and a commitment to ensure all kids are in school. Realizing steady improvements also comes down to national and international commitment, political leadership, and an emphasis on tailoring policies to local circumstances to meet the distinct challenges each country faces. Serious efforts, even in countries with highly constrained resources, are likely to yield impressive results, both for educational outcomes and for the society as a whole. In short, there may be no better investment for the health and development of poor countries around the world than investments to educate girls.

I. The State of Girls' Education Today

A cross the developing world, tens of millions of girls are not getting a basic education. In recent years this crisis, which is particularly acute in rural and poor areas of sub-Saharan Africa, the Middle East, and South Asia, has attracted increased public attention. More than 180 nations have committed to addressing this challenge by pledging that every boy and girl will receive a quality basic education by 2015. This target is now firmly established and endorsed as one of the eight United Nations Millennium Development Goals.

Yet to reach the goal of universal education for children, policymakers will need to make special efforts to address the economic, social, and cultural barriers that keep large numbers of girls in poor countries out of school. Indeed, extensive research confirms that investing in girls' education delivers high returns not only for female educational attainment, but also for mothers' and children's health, sustainable families, women's empowerment, democracy, income growth, and productivity.

- **104 million children ages 6–11 are not in school each year—60 million are girls.** Nearly 40 percent of these out-of-school children live in sub-Saharan Africa; 35 percent live in South Asia.

  UNESCO. 2003. *Education for All Global Monitoring Report 2003/4.* Paris: UNESCO.

- **Studies find that 150 million children currently enrolled in school will drop out before completing primary school—at least 100 million are girls.** In many countries, simply getting kids into classrooms does not guarantee that they will stay. Getting children to complete, not just attend, school is of critical importance. A recent World Bank report found that in Africa, "a majority of adults with less than five or six years of primary schooling remain functionally illiterate and innumerate throughout their lives."

World Bank. 2002. "Education for Dynamic Economies: Action Plan to Accelerate Progress towards Education for All (EFA)." Washington, D.C.: World Bank.

- ◆ **Only 36 of the 155 developing countries have achieved 100 percent primary school completion rates.**

  World Bank. 2002. "Education for Dynamic Economies: Action Plan to Accelerate Progress towards Education for All (EFA)." Washington, D.C.: World Bank.

- ◆ **The gender gap in primary school completion is greater than 10 percentage points.** The United Nations Children's Fund (UNICEF) emphasizes that "this yawning gender gap means that millions more girls than boys are dropping out each year."

  UNICEF. 2003. *State of the World's Children 2004.* New York: UNICEF.

- • **In Africa, more than half of girls—54 percent—do not complete even a primary school education (see Figure 1).**

  Bruns, Barbara, Alain Mingat, and Ramahatra Rakotomalala. 2003. "Achieving Universal Primary Education by 2015: A Chance for Every Child." Washington, D.C.: World Bank.

- ◆ **In Chad, 89 percent of all 15- to 19-year-old girls had not completed primary school, and in Burkina Faso 80 percent had not done so, according to a 1999 study.** More than 90 percent of 15- to 19-year-old girls from the bottom 40 percent of households in a number of countries, including Mali, Niger, and Burkina Faso, had not completed even first grade.

  Filmer, Deon. 1999. "The Structure of Social Disparities in Education: Gender and Wealth." Policy Research Report on Gender and Development, Working Paper Series No. 5, World Bank Development Research Group/Poverty and Human Resources. Washington, D.C.: World Bank. May.

- • **In South Asia, more than 40 percent of 15- to 19-year-old girls from poor households never completed even first grade, and only one in four completed fifth grade, according to a 1999 study.**

  Filmer, Deon, and Lant Pritchett. 1999. "The Effect of Household Wealth on Educational Attainment." *Population and Development Review* 25 (1): 85–120.

- • **Beyond primary school, girls' participation plummets further: only 17 percent of girls in Africa are enrolled in secondary school.**

  UNESCO. 2003. *Education for All Global Monitoring Report 2003/4.* Paris: UNESCO.

- ◆ **In Cambodia, only 12 percent of girls enroll in secondary school, and in Laos fewer than one in four girls attend beyond the primary level.**

  UNESCO. 2003. *Regional Report on South and East Asia.* Paris: UNESCO Institute for Statistics.

- • **The difference between urban and rural areas is striking, especially for girls.**

FIGURE **1**

In Africa, Fewer than 50 Percent of Girls Complete Primary School
In South Asia, Girls Lag Far Behind Boys

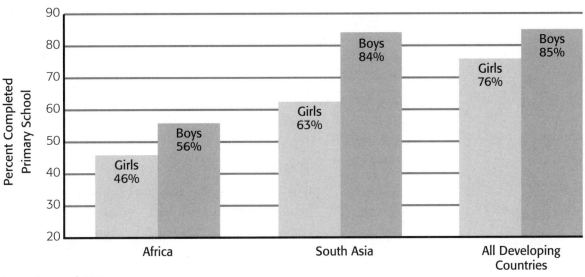

Source: Bruns et al. 2003.

♦ **In Niger, 83 percent of girls in the capital of Niamey were enrolled in primary school, compared to 12 percent enrolled in rural areas, according to a 1996 study.**

World Bank. 1996. "Niger Poverty Assessment: A Resilient People in a Harsh Environment." Washington, D.C.: World Bank. Cited in Oxfam, "Education Report," 2001.

♦ **In Pakistan, the primary school completion rate for boys in rural areas is three times higher than for girls, while in urban areas it is just twice as high.**

Government of Pakistan. 1997. "Pakistan Integrated Household Survey: Round 1 1995–1996." Islamabad. Cited in Oxfam, "Education Report," 2001.

• **At least one in three girls completing primary school in Africa and South Asia cannot effectively read, write, or do simple arithmetic.**

♦ **Education quality lags far behind in many Arab countries, even those with strong resources.** A major report by the United Nations Development Programme (UNDP) concluded that in the region, "education policies lack an integrated vision of the education process." A study in Bahrain showed that in math, the average grade was just 45 percent, with a wide range in performance.

UNDP. 2003. *Arab Human Development Report 2003.* New York: UNDP.

◆ **In Egypt, a study found final reading and writing scores on national exams were about half of mastery level.** In Pakistan, pass rates on national exams at the end of primary school have been set at 30 percent because few children are expected to do better.

> Fredriksen, Birger. 2002. "Education for All Children by 2015: What Will It Take to Keep the Promise?" Paper presented at the World Bank Annual Conference on Development Economics. Oslo. June 24–26.

> World Bank. 1996. "Improving Basic Education in Pakistan." Report 14960-PAK. Washington, D.C.: World Bank.

◆ **The gender gap in achievement remains stark: in Azerbaijan, only 52 percent of girls passed post-primary reading and math tests, compared to 100 percent of boys.**

> UNICEF. 2003. *State of the World's Children 2004.* New York: UNICEF.

◆ **Moreover, what children do learn may be worrisome.** In some countries, schools can help perpetuate gender stereotypes, which discourage girls' achievement, and may promote ethnic, religious, or political stereotypes that may encourage intolerance or even conflict and violence.

> UNDP. 2001. *Human Development Report 2001.* Oxford: Oxford University Press.

• **UNICEF has identified 25 countries where "girls' education will be treated as a case for urgent—even emergency—action." Of the 25 countries chosen, 10 have more than 1 million girls out of school.**

> UNICEF. 2003. *State of the World's Children 2004.* New York: UNICEF.

II. The Impact of Educating Girls: The Evidence

Extensive evidence from developing countries in widely different circumstances shows that education, especially of girls, has enormous economic and social benefits; it is one of the soundest investments any country can make. Evidence on the returns to girls' education falls into four broad categories:

- **Increased Income and Productivity.** Education generally leads to increased income and productivity, for individuals and for nations as a whole. Although women often start from a weaker economic position than men, evidence shows that educating girls generally produces greater gains in productivity and income than educating boys, and educating girls has as much or more impact on national economic growth.

- **Smaller, Healthier, Better-Educated Families.** A strong and extensive body of evidence confirms that educating women is the single most effective way to encourage smaller, healthier, and better-educated families.

- **HIV/AIDS and Other Disease Prevention.** Evidence is increasingly showing that education can be one of the best defenses against HIV/AIDS, both because of education's impact on women's earning capacity, empowerment, and family well-being, and because school-based HIV education programs discourage risky behavior among young girls in particular.

- **Women's Empowerment.** A growing body of research suggests that education helps empower women to stand up for themselves and their children. By changing women's "bargaining position" in both the family and society, education can bring benefits not only to women and their children, but to the broader community and society, such as through more effective and representative governance.

A. Education and Income Growth

1. Higher Wages

Extensive research has shown that both primary and secondary education produce high returns in terms of wage growth, whether for men or for women. The returns to primary education have long been established, but more recent research has shown substantial benefits to secondary education as well, particularly as economies advance and modernize. Studies vary in quality and coverage, and methodological debates remain. But in terms of future workforce participation, the body of research literature indicates that the overall returns of educating women—whether they attend primary or secondary schools—are even higher than for men.

- **World Bank studies have concluded that an extra year of education beyond the average boosts girls' eventual wages by 10–20 percent.** A recent cross-country study found returns to primary education averaging 5–15 percent for boys and slightly higher for girls. The study concluded that "overall, women receive higher returns to their schooling investments."

    Psacharopoulos, George, and Harry Anthony Patrinos. 2002. "Returns to Investment in Education: A Further Update." World Bank Policy Research Working Paper 2881. Washington, D.C.: World Bank.

    Psacharopoulos, George. 1994. "Returns to Investment in Education: A Global Update." *World Development* 22 (9): 1325–43.

- **A leading development economist has found returns to female secondary education in the 15–25 percent range.** Through extensive analysis with careful adjustment for various research methods, Yale economist Paul Schultz has found that wage gains from education tend to be similar if not somewhat higher for women than for men, and that the returns to secondary education in particular are appreciably higher for women. He concluded in a recent paper, "Increasing investments in women's human capital, especially education, should be a priority for countries seeking both economic growth and human welfare." "The case for directing educational investment to women is stronger," Schultz added, "the greater the initial disparity in investments between men and women."

    Schultz, T. Paul. 2002. "Why Governments Should Invest More to Educate Girls." *World Development* 30 (2): 207–25.

    Schultz, T. Paul. 1993. "Returns to Women's Schooling." In Elizabeth King and M. Anne Hill, eds., *Women's Education in Developing Countries: Barriers, Benefits, and Policy.* Baltimore: Johns Hopkins University Press.

    Schultz, T. Paul. 1992. "Investments in Schooling and Health of Women and Men: Quantities and Returns." Paper prepared for Conference on Women's Human Capital and Development, Bellagio, Italy. May.

    See also Schultz, T. Paul. 1995. *Investment in Women's Human Capital.* Chicago: University of Chicago Press.

- **Educated women are more likely to enter the formal labor market, where they often reap greater wage gains than in the informal sector.** In Brazil and Guinea, the greater women's schooling, the less likely they are to work in the informal and domestic sectors, which pay low or even subsistence wages. By facilitating the transition from the informal to the formal sector, education provides the opportunity for significant and sustained income gains.

  Malhotra, Anju, Caren Grown, and Rohini Pande. 2003. "Impact of Investments in Female Education on Gender Inequality." Washington, D.C.: International Center for Research on Women.

2. Faster Economic Growth

Research to demonstrate the link between girls' education and economic growth is complex, but carefully done cross-country studies controlling for a variety of other influences find that female education promotes per capita income growth.

- **Increasing the share of women with secondary education by 1 percentage point boosts annual per capita income growth by 0.3 percentage points on average, according to a 100-country study by the World Bank.** Such a difference means a lot, as few countries achieve per capita income growth beyond 3 percent annually, and incomes are falling in parts of Africa. The study concludes that "societies that have a preference for not investing in girls pay a price for it in terms of slower growth and reduced income" (see Box 1).

  Dollar, David, and Roberta Gatti. 1999. "Gender Inequality, Income, and Growth: Are Good Times Good for Women?" World Bank Policy Research Report on Gender and Development, Working Paper Series No. 1. Washington, D.C.: World Bank.

- **It is not just the level of female education that matters for economic growth: a World Bank study found that the education gender gap has held back annual per capita growth by nearly 1 percent a year.** The analysis found that, had South Asia and sub-Saharan Africa started with more equal education levels for men and women in 1960 and done more to close the gender gap during 1960–92, their per capita income growth could have been as much as 0.9 percent per year higher. The study concludes, "Promoting gender equity in education and employment may be one of those few policies that have been termed 'win-win' strategies" (see Box 2).

  Klasen, Stephan. 1999. "Does Gender Inequality Reduce Growth and Development? Evidence from Cross-Country Regressions." Policy Research Report on Gender and Development Working Paper No. 7. Washington, D.C.: World Bank.

- **Education leads to, and does not just accompany, economic growth.** Although this link has long been known in East Asia, it appears in other regions too. The impact of math and science education on growth is particularly strong. This study does not, however, distinguish between male and female education.

  Hanushek, Erik A., and Dennis D. Kimko. 2000. "Schooling, Labor Force Quality, and the Growth of Nations." *American Economic Review* 90 (5): 1184–208.

BOX **1**

Female Education and Development Can Reinforce Each Other

A 100-country World Bank study found that the gender gap in education disappears with development, while efforts to educate girls boost the pace of development and in turn promote education—a virtuous cycle. In the poorest quartile of countries in 1990, 5 percent of women had secondary education, about one-half the level for men. In the richest quartile, male and female education levels were higher and similar: 38 percent for women and 39 percent for men. As per capita income grows, girls' enrollments catch up with boys', slowly until countries reach lower-middle-income levels and faster thereafter. But poverty alone does not explain the gender gap in education; it also varies with religion, region, and civil liberties.

Increasing girls' education—controlling for other influences—creates a better environment for economic growth, particularly as developing countries move into middle-income levels. Increasing the share of women with secondary education by 1 percentage point boosts annual per capita income growth by 0.3 percentage points. The study suggests that deliberate efforts to educate girls, particularly where barriers to female education exist, can help shift the development process into higher gear.

Dollar, David, and Roberta Gatti. 1999. "Gender Inequality, Income, and Growth: Are Good Times Good for Women?" World Bank Policy Research Report on Gender and Development, Working Paper Series No. 1. Washington, D.C.: World Bank.

3. More Productive Farming

Research in this area is limited but suggests that both male and female farmers can raise their productivity and efficiency if they have greater access to education, technology, and farming resources. Yet because female farmers tend to begin with less access to all of these things, agricultural productivity rises substantially when women can catch up. The result is not only higher incomes but higher production of food and other consumable goods.

- **A recent 63-country study by the International Food Policy Research Institute (IFPRI) found that more productive farming due to increased female education accounts for 43 percent of the decline in malnutrition achieved between 1970 and 1995.**

    Smith, Lisa C., and Lawrence Haddad. 1999. "Explaining Child Malnutrition in Developing Countries: A Cross-Country Analysis." IFPRI Food Consumption and Nutrition Division Discussion Paper 60. Washington, D.C.: IFPRI.

- **A Kenyan study found that the lack of girls' education depresses farm productivity.** The same study showed that if women farmers in Kenya had the same education and input levels as men farmers, yields could rise by 22 percent.

    Quisumbing, Agnes. 1996. "Male-Female Differences in Agricultural Productivity: Methodological Issues and Empirical Evidence." *World Development* 24 (10): 1579–95.

- **A classic earlier study in East Africa established that education helped both women and men farmers increase their efficiency and productivity, controlling for other influences.**

  Jamison, Dean, and Lawrence J. Lau. 1982. *Farmer Education and Farm Efficiency.* Baltimore: Johns Hopkins University Press.

- **Another study of African countries found that women farmers are a critical target group: their generally low levels of education mean higher potential productivity gains from providing them access to education and other endowments.** Women account for three-fourths of all food produced in sub-Saharan Africa, yet women heading farm households have not only lower educational attainments than men, but also lower educational attainments than other women. In Nigeria, women heading households had, on average, 1.6 years of education, compared to 3.0 years for men and 2.5 years for all women surveyed. Therefore women farmers represent an especially important target group for increased education to raise overall agricultural productivity.

  Saito, Katrine, Hailu Mekonen, and Daphne Spurling, 1994. "Raising the Productivity of Women Farmers in Sub-Saharan Africa." World Bank Discussion Paper No. 230. Washington, D.C.: World Bank.

BOX **2**

Reducing the Gender Gap in Education Promotes Economic Growth

Annual growth in per capita income from 1960–92 was slowest in sub-Saharan Africa, averaging 0.7 percent annually—about one-third the world average. The education gender gap in 1960 was high in Africa (women had only about half as much education as men), and African women saw the slowest education growth of any region in the world from 1960 to 1992. In sharp contrast, East Asia saw growth of over 4 percent between 1960 and 1992, and over that period, women's education increased three times as fast as in Africa and 44 percent faster than it increased for East Asian men—leading to a closing of the education gender gap in the region.

Controlling for other factors, the disparity in the education gender gaps between Africa and East Asia accounts for 16 percent of the difference in economic growth over the 1960–92 period. About one-third of this difference is attributable to the existing gender gaps in 1960, and two-thirds to the divergent progress on addressing the gaps between 1960 and 1992. Likewise, the disparity in education gender gaps between East Asia and South Asia accounts for 40 percent of the difference in economic growth between the two regions, with about 55 percent of this difference stemming from the existing gaps in 1960 and 45 percent from changes in the gaps over time.

Klasen, Stephan. 1999. "Does Gender Inequality Reduce Growth and Development? Evidence from Cross-Country Regressions." Policy Research Report on Gender and Development Working Paper No. 7. Washington, D.C.: World Bank.

B. Education and Smaller, Healthier, Better-Educated Families

A wealth of cross-country and individual country studies from Africa, Asia, and Latin America over the past 25 years reveals a pattern: women with more education have smaller, healthier, and better-educated families. As education opens up better opportunities for women to earn, and as it changes women's position in the family and society, couples tend to opt for smaller families—and to invest more in the health and education of each child. Fertility declines among educated women for several reasons: they generally marry later (often in their twenties rather than their teens); they have more opportunities available to them to earn income outside the home; they have more influence in family decisions; and they are better able to use contraceptives.

Consequently, female education is widely regarded as a critical influence on family size and population trends (see Figure 2). Of course, providing good family planning services is also critical, so that people can safely have the number of children they want. Finally, recent research suggests that, as with economic gains, it is not just years of female education that matter, but whether women have as much education as men. As women catch up, the positive impact on family size and family well-being tends to grow.

1. Educating Girls Leads to Smaller, More Sustainable Families

Extensive evidence from many countries shows that, controlling for other influences, when women are educated, couples tend to choose to have substantially fewer children.

- **Doubling the proportion of women with a secondary education would reduce average fertility rates from 5.3 to 3.9 children per woman.** This rigorous cross-country analysis looked at fertility and secondary school attainment among women in 65 low- and middle-income countries in 1985, collectively including 93 percent of the population of the developing world (see Box 3).

- **The same study concluded that "the expansion of female secondary education may be the best single policy for achieving substantial reductions in fertility."**

     Subbarao, K., and Laura Raney. 1995. "Social Gains from Female Education." *Economic Development and Cultural Change* 44 (1): 105–28.

- **A 100-country study found that when women gain four years more education on average, the fertility rate per woman drops by almost one birth.** This study controls for other influences on fertility, such as income, children's mortality rates, and regional differences, and concludes that fertility falls by almost one birth per woman for every four years beyond the average of women's

FIGURE **2**

Post-Primary Education Leads to Dramatic Declines in Fertility

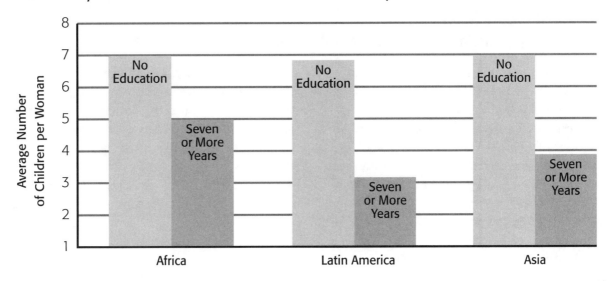

Source: Schultz 1993.

schooling. But it is not just years of female education that matter. The greater the gap between men's and women's education, the higher the fertility rate. In fact, the gender gap matters more than women's overall level of education in determining fertility rates.

> Klasen, Stephan. 1999. "Does Gender Inequality Reduce Growth and Development? Evidence from Cross-Country Regressions." Policy Research Report on Gender and Development Working Paper No. 7. Washington, D.C.: World Bank.

- **Many individual country studies in Africa, Asia, and Latin America reveal the same pattern. A study in Brazil found that illiterate women have an average of 6 children each, whereas literate women have an average of 2.5 children.** The main exception to this trend is in the Middle East, where even educated women may be isolated within their communities and from the labor force and broader society.

> UNESCO. 2000. "Women and Girls: Education, Not Discrimination." Paris: UNESCO.

> World Bank. 2001. *Engendering Development.* World Bank Policy Research Report. Washington, D.C., and Oxford: World Bank and Oxford University Press.

> Lloyd, C. B., C. E. Kaufman, and P. Hewett. 2000. "The Spread of Primary Schooling in Sub-Saharan Africa: Implications for Fertility Change." *Population and Development Review* 26 (3): 483–515.

BOX 3

Female Education Promotes Lower Fertility and Mortality Simultaneously

A multicountry study, recently confirmed, shows that female secondary education reduces fertility and mortality as a package. The study covered 65 low- and middle-income countries in 1985, including 93 percent of the population of the developing world. In countries where few women had a secondary education, family size averaged more than five children, of whom one or two died in infancy. But in countries where half the girls were educated at the secondary level, the fertility rate fell to just over three children and child deaths were rare. In these 65 countries, doubling the proportion of girls educated at the secondary level from 19 percent to 38 percent in 1985, holding constant all other variables (including access to family planning and health care), would have cut the fertility rate from 5.3 to 3.9 and the infant mortality rate from 81 to 38 babies per 1,000. In percentage terms, it would have reduced births by 29 percent and infant deaths by 64 percent, compared to the actual in 1985.

Subbarao, K., and Laura Raney. 1995. "Social Gains from Female Education." *Economic Development and Cultural Change* 44(1): 105–28.

---

2. Educating Women Saves Children's Lives

Extensive research across and within diverse countries has established that female education—controlling for other influences—strikingly decreases infant mortality. The mother's education is often the single most important influence on children's survival. Recent research shows that better maternal education is associated with better height and body mass indicators for children. Primary education alone helps reduce infant mortality significantly, and secondary education helps even more.

Education helps mothers learn what their children need to stay healthy and how to secure necessary supports for their children—by using health services, improving nutrition and sanitation, and taking advantage of their own increased earning capability. Girls who stay in school also marry later, when they are better able to bear and care for children.

- **A Yale economist found that an extra year of girls' education cuts infant mortality 5–10 percent.** His review of many country studies found that each additional year of a mother's schooling cuts the expected infant mortality rate by an average of 5–10 percent. This link "is especially striking in low income countries. The pattern has been widely replicated across comparative data bases . . . and through repeated censuses."

  Schultz, T. Paul. 1993. "Returns to Women's Schooling." In Elizabeth King and M. Anne Hill, eds., *Women's Education in Developing Countries: Barriers, Benefits, and Policy.* Baltimore: Johns Hopkins University Press.

- **Educating girls for five years could boost child survival by up to 40 percent in Africa.** An analysis of African data by then-World Bank chief economist Lawrence Summers revealed that children born to mothers who had received five years of primary education were on average 40 percent more likely to survive to age five.

   > Summers, Lawrence H. 1994. "Investing in All the People: Educating Women in Developing Countries." EDI Seminar Paper No. 45. Washington, D.C.: World Bank.

- **Infant mortality is one-quarter lower where girls are educated as much as boys are, according a World Bank study in Africa.** The wider the education gender gap, the greater the under-five mortality rate tends to be in the developing world—especially in Africa. Africa's under-five mortality rate in 1990 would have been more than one-quarter lower (167 versus 122 deaths per 1,000 births) after controlling for income, schooling, and other differences if Africa had had rough parity between male and female education.

   > Klasen, Stephan. 1999. "Does Gender Inequality Reduce Growth and Development? Evidence from Cross-Country Regressions." Policy Research Report on Gender and Development Working Paper No. 7. Washington, D.C.: World Bank.

- **Multicountry data show that educated mothers are about 50 percent more likely to immunize their children than are uneducated mothers.** This trend holds in both Africa and South Asia, the two regions where most of the world's uneducated girls are found. Recent demographic data in Africa show that half the children of mothers with a primary education are immunized, compared with over one-third of those whose mothers had no education. In South Asia, fewer than 30 percent of children of mothers with no education were immunized, compared with over 40 percent of those whose mothers had a primary education. While part of this effect is accounted for by household incomes, maternal education strongly predicts immunization rates even in comparable households.

   > Gage, Anastasia, Elisabeth Sommerfelt, and Andrea Piani. 1997. "Household Structure and Childhood Immunization in Niger and Nigeria." *Demography* 34 (2): 195–309.

- **Where only half as many girls as boys go to school, 21 more children per 1,000 die.** This cross-country analysis of development indicators found that countries where girls are only half as likely as boys are to go to school have on average about 21 more infant deaths per 1,000 live births than countries with no gender gap, controlling for average levels of income and education.

   - ◆ **The study also finds that increasing girls' enrollment by 10 percent saves more than 4 children per 1,000.** Increasing girls' enrollment in primary and secondary school by 10 percent is associated with an average decline in infant mortality of 4.1 and 5.6 deaths per 1,000 births, respectively.

      > Hill, M. Anne, and Elizabeth King. 1995. "Women's Education and Economic Well-Being." *Feminist Economics* 1 (2): 21–46.

3. Educating Women Helps Educate the Next Generation

Studies in different countries confirm that both maternal and paternal education affect children's educational attainment, but on the whole, evidence shows that having an educated mother helps ensure that children go to school longer and study more.

- **Women's education generally has more impact than men's education on children's schooling, a recent multicountry study found.** In 14 countries, including Brazil, Chad, India, Pakistan, the Philippines, and Uganda, female education had more impact than male education. On the whole, increasing women's education by one year beyond the average level boosted the probability of children's enrollment in schools by 1–6 percentage points. Among countries with a large female disadvantage in enrollment, the education of adult women generally has more impact on the enrollment of girls than on that of boys—such as in Cameroon, India, Pakistan, and Turkey. In several other countries, however, women's education has more impact on boys (such as in Bangladesh and much of Africa and Latin America).

  Filmer, Deon. 2000. "The Structure of Social Disparities in Education: Gender and Wealth." Policy Research Working Paper No. 2268, World Bank Development Research Group/Poverty Reduction and Economic Management Network. Washington, D.C.: World Bank.

- **A study in India found that children of educated women study two extra hours per day.** A recent study of India during the Green Revolution found that children whose mothers were more educated studied two hours more each day on average than did children with uneducated mothers in otherwise similar households.

  Behrman, Jere, et al. 1999. "Women's Schooling, Home Teaching, and Economic Growth." *Journal of Political Economy* 107 (4): 682–719.

- **Multiple studies have found that a mother's level of education has a strong positive effect on her daughters' enrollment—more than on sons' and significantly more than the effect of fathers' education on daughters.** Studies from Ghana, Egypt, Kenya, Peru, and Malaysia all find that mothers with a basic education are substantially more likely to educate their children, and especially their daughters, even controlling for other influences. Paternal education also promotes children's enrollment, more for girls than for boys, but the effects of maternal education are stronger.

  Lavy, Victor. 1996. "School Supply Constraints and Children's Educational Outcomes in Rural Ghana." *Journal of Development Economics* 51 (2): 291–314.

  Ridker, Ronald G., ed. 1997. "Determinants of Educational Achievement and Attainment in Africa: Findings from Nine Case Studies." SD Publication Series, Technical Paper No. 62. Washington, D.C.: U.S. Agency for International Development.

  King, Elizabeth, and Rosemary Bellew. 1991. "Gains in the Education of Peruvian Women, 1940–1980." In Barbara Herz and Shahidur Khandkher, eds., "Women's

Work, Education, and Family Welfare in Peru." World Bank Discussion Paper No. 116. Washington, D.C.: World Bank.

Alderman, Harold, and Elizabeth M. King. 1998. "Gender Differences in Parental Investment in Education." *Structural Change and Economic Dynamics* 9 (4): 453–68.

C. Education and HIV/AIDS

Some 42 million people around the world are living with HIV/AIDS. Moreover, projections suggest that unless dramatic steps are taken, an additional 45 million will become infected before 2010. In Africa, 58 percent of the 29.4 million infected people are women.

HIV is spreading faster among teenage girls than in any other group, primarily through sexual relationships with older men. In a number of African countries, five to six girls in the 15- to 19-year-old age range are infected for every one boy. In some countries, an astounding half of the young women now alive may well die of HIV/AIDS.

More than half of the countries that are not on track to reach the goal of universal primary education are also those worst affected by HIV/AIDS. The impact of the disease on girls' schooling is more acute in countries with the highest HIV prevalence rates, where girls' enrollments are declining due to care-giving responsibilities or their own infection. Girls' enrollments are more stable in countries with lower prevalence rates. Yet lacking a vaccine for the virus or a cure for the disease, education is the single best way to prevent the spread of HIV/AIDS. Although half of all new HIV infections are among 15- to 24-year-olds, prevalence rates are lowest among those in the 5–14 age group. This generation of young people provides what Don Bundy and other experts at the World Bank call a "window of hope" for preventing the spread of HIV/AIDS.

> World Bank. 2002. "Education and HIV/AIDS: A Window of Hope." World Bank Education Section, Human Development Department. Washington, D.C.: World Bank.

> UNAIDS. 2003. "HIV/AIDS Epidemic Update 2003." New York: UNAIDS. December.

1. Educated Girls Are Less Likely to Contract HIV

In the 1980s, early in the AIDS pandemic, HIV infection rates tended to be higher among more-educated people, which researchers think was because the adult generation at that time had been educated before HIV/AIDS struck and because more-educated people tended to have higher incomes and were more mobile. In the 1990s, however, things changed. Today, an increasing body of research shows that more-educated people, especially youth, are less likely to engage in risky behavior and contract HIV.

- **Women with post-primary education are five times more likely than illiterate women to know the basic facts about HIV/AIDS, according to a 32-country review of demographic and health surveys.** Illiterate women are three times more likely to think that a healthy-looking person cannot be HIV positive and four times more likely to believe that there is no way to avoid AIDS.

    Vandemoortele, J., and E. Delamonica. 2000. "Education 'Vaccine' against HIV/AIDS." *Current Issues in Comparative Education* 3 (1).

- **A study of 72 countries has found that HIV prevalence reaches the outbreak level of 5 percent in countries where the literacy gap exceeds 25 percentage points between boys and girls. By contrast, HIV prevalence rates fall to 3 percent where the literacy gap between boys and girls is below 5 percent.** The study analyzed low-risk urban adults in 72 countries and controlled for other influences.

    Over, Mead. 1998. "The Effects of Societal Variables on Urban Rates of HIV Infection in Developing Countries: An Exploratory Analysis." In Martha Ainsworth, Lieve Fransen, and Mead Over, eds., *Confronting AIDS: Evidence from the Developing World.* Brussels and Washington, D.C.: European Commission and World Bank.

- **A Zambian study found that AIDS spreads twice as fast among uneducated girls.** During the 1990s, HIV infection rates for uneducated women stayed constant while HIV infection rates among educated women fell by half, suggesting that educated women may be better able to defend themselves against HIV infection.

    Vandemoortele, J., and E. Delamonica. 2000. "Education 'Vaccine' against HIV/AIDS." *Current Issues in Comparative Education* 3 (1).

- **Young rural Ugandans with secondary-level education are three times less likely to be HIV positive than young Ugandans with no education.** A recent study found that during the 1990s, young people who had some secondary schooling were three times less likely to be HIV positive, and those who had some primary schooling were about half as likely as those who received no schooling to be HIV positive. One additional year of education decreases the probability of contracting HIV by 6.7 percent.

    De Walque, Damien. 2004. "How Does Educational Attainment Affect the Risk of Being Infected by HIV/AIDS? Evidence from a General Population Cohort in Rural Uganda." World Bank Development Research Group Working Paper. Washington, D.C.: World Bank. March.

- **A Kenyan study found that girls who stay in school are four times more likely to delay sexual activity.** The study found that among 17- to 18-year-old girls, those who were in school were almost four times as likely to be virgins as those who were out of school.

    UNICEF. 2002. "Education and HIV Prevention." Citing data from Kenya Demographic and Health Survey. New York: UNICEF.

- **Women with at least a primary education are three times more likely than uneducated women to know that HIV can be transmitted from mother to child.**

  World Bank. 2002. "Education and HIV/AIDS: A Window of Hope." World Bank Education Section, Human Development Department. Washington, D.C.: World Bank.

- **Education helps women protect against the risk of HIV infection by reducing risky behaviors and increasing a woman's ability to discuss sex with a partner and negotiate behaviors, such as condom use, that reduce risk,** according to a recent review of research that examined several studies of HIV/AIDS in Africa and Latin America. Education's impact is stronger in urban areas and where violence against women is less prevalent.

  Malhotra, Anju, Caren Grown, and Rohini Pande. 2003. "Impact of Investments in Female Education on Gender Inequality." Washington, D.C.: International Center for Research on Women.

2. School-Based Education Programs Help Prevent HIV Infection

Schools provide a ready-made infrastructure to reach the world's children with education to change behavior before they become infected. Unfortunately, HIV/AIDS is also undermining education systems and pulling children, especially girls, out of school. In Zimbabwe, for example, a study of five provinces found that more than three-fourths of the children pulled out of school to care for relatives with AIDS are young girls. In these circumstances, it is critical to attack HIV/AIDS and work to preserve and improve the school system simultaneously, incorporating education on HIV/AIDS as a critical part of teaching.

The UNAIDS Inter-Agency Task Team on Education and HIV/AIDS emphasizes another aspect of the problem: "Women and girls are made vulnerable to HIV/AIDS because of the greater power that men and boys generally have in sexual relations. The education sector—and the classroom in particular—have a key role to play in engaging young people in rethinking gender roles and in the process reducing the risk of HIV/AIDS." UNAIDS adds, "Education is an effective, proven weapon against HIV/AIDS. Unfortunately, HIV/AIDS is very effective in attacking the very fabric of the education system. Thus working to preserve the core functions of education and educating to prevent spread of the disease are complementary and inseparable."

UNESCO. 2002. *Gender, Education, and HIV/AIDS.* Instituto Promundo. Rio de Janeiro: UNESCO.

UNESCO. 2002. "Press Release for *A Strategic Approach: HIV/AIDS and Education.*" Available at http://portal.unesco.org/ev.php?URL.

Sperling, Gene. 2003. "School Is the Front Line Against AIDS." *International Herald Tribune.* May 28.

- **A review of 113 studies from five continents found that school-based AIDS education programs that focus on specific, age-appropriate behavioral objectives are effective in reducing early sexual activity and high-risk behavior.** School-based prevention presents an especially promising opportunity to prevent the spread of AIDS, because schools offer a captive audience of uninfected children just before they move into the age bracket where infection becomes most likely.

   Kirby, D., et al. 1994. "School-Based Programs to Reduce Risk Behaviors: A Review of Effectiveness." *Public Health Reports* 109 (3): 339–61.

- **School-based AIDS education in Uganda reduced risky behavior by 75 percent.** A controlled two-year study of a school-based intervention program found that, of students in their last year of primary school who had been exposed to the program, only 11 percent were sexually active, compared to 43 percent of students who received only standard health education.

   Shuey, D. A., et al. 1999. "Increased Sexual Abstinence among In-School Adolescents as a Result of School Health Education in Soroti District, Uganda." *Health Education Research* 14 (3): 411–19.

- **Programs in Africa targeting younger primary school students have had greater success in influencing sexual behaviors than those targeting secondary school students.** A review of 11 studies of school-based HIV-prevention programs for youth in sub-Saharan Africa found that it is easier to establish low-risk behaviors and build knowledge around prevention among younger students who have not had their sexual debut. The review also indicates that school-based programs are most effective in their ability to increase and sustain condom use—both among virgins and among youth who are sexually active.

   Gallant, M., and E. Maticka-Tyndale. 2003. "School-Based HIV Prevention Programmes for African Youth." *Social Science and Medicine* 58 (7): 337–51 .

- **A pilot program of innovative, school-based AIDS prevention approaches in Mwanza, Tanzania, produced dramatic improvement in HIV/AIDS knowledge and reported attitudes.** The project, implemented in partnership with the Tanzanian government, the African Medical Research Foundation, and the London School of Hygiene and Tropical Medicine, relies on existing teachers, schools, and health workers and employs innovative, locally appropriate techniques to affect behavior through drama, peer-led lessons, stories, and games. A rigorous evaluation of the pilot phase, conducted from 1999 to 2001, found the program to be extremely popular, with teacher reports demonstrating that more than 80 percent of the lessons were taught and annual exams revealing a dramatic improvement in pupils' knowledge and reported attitudes related to sexual and reproductive health in the pilot communities. Some sexual behaviors changed as well.

   Ross, David. 2003. "Results from a Community Randomized Trial in Rural Tanzania: MEMA kwa Vijana Project." Presentation to the Conference on New Findings from Intervention Research: Youth Reproductive Health and Youth HIV Prevention. Washington, D.C. September 9.

D. Education and Empowered Women

Nobel laureate Amartya Sen emphasizes that education helps empower women within the family and society. As that happens, women not only improve their own welfare, but through their "agency," act to improve the well-being of their children and help transform society itself (see Box 4).

This empowerment of women comes from greater years of education, but it also comes as women catch up with men in education even when average levels of education remain quite low. That is why years of female education and parity between men and women both affect economic gains, changes in family size, and improvements in children's health and education. The empowering effects of education for women also show up dramatically for women themselves, by reducing violence against women and helping them stand up to threats such as HIV/AIDS.

1. Female Education Can Reduce Domestic Violence

In poor areas where women are isolated within their communities, have little education, and cannot earn much, girls are often regarded as an economic burden, and women and girls sometimes suffer deliberate neglect or outright harm. A 50-country

---

BOX **4**

Women's Empowerment and HIV/AIDS

As explained above, the HIV infection rate in many developing countries is growing fastest among teenage girls. This is the result of both young girls engaging in risky behavior, often with older men, and girls being subjected to different forms of sexual coercion, from outright rape to intimidation. Whether in Africa, Asia, or Latin America, and even in some higher-income countries, thousands of uneducated women and girls (some as young as ten) are forced into prostitution for lack of earning opportunities. The result is often not only rampant HIV/AIDS among them, but also transmission of the disease to men and to other uninfected spouses or partners. Other uneducated young women may enter casual sexual relationships with older men whom they cannot easily oppose, with obvious implications for further spread of the disease.

While people may differ in their reading of the level of coercion along this spectrum, education for girls is a critical tool in knowing how to avoid risks and change power dynamics in sexual relationships. Girls who attend school are far more likely to understand the dangers involved in risky behavior, not believe the myths associated with sex, and (in the case of good school health programs) even know effective refusal tactics in difficult sexual situations. Equally as important, education helps girls gain the economic clout and the standing in society to avoid high-risk behaviors and save their own lives. While education is not a foolproof solution to sexual violence and the transmission of HIV/AIDS, it is widely seen as the most fundamental contributor to giving women more voice and standing in their families and communities.

study has found that 16–50 percent of women have been victims of physical violence, mainly from family members.

- **Although reducing domestic violence involves complicated social change, some research suggests that when women gain education, earning capacity, and standing in society, this neglect gives way.** Girls are allowed more equal access to food and health care. The age of marriage rises beyond the early teen years and pregnancies are more widely spaced. And women can better seek health care for themselves, and are better able to protect themselves from threats such as HIV/AIDS (see Box 4). In general, female education is more effective in reducing violence against women where social norms already allow women more voice and choice in their own lives, and education can help change those norms.

    Sen, Amartya. 2000. *Development as Freedom.* New York: Anchor Books.

    Heise, Lori, Mary Elsberg, and Megan Gottemoeller. 1999. "Ending Violence against Women." Population Reports L (11), Population Information Program. Baltimore: Johns Hopkins University School of Public Health.

- **Women with no formal schooling are less likely to resist violence and to leave abusive relationships than women with some schooling.** Controlling for other influences, education does deter violence. Several studies in India, including a 1992 survey of 1,300 women ranging from adolescence to middle age, show that whether women have had some schooling can affect the probability of being beaten, and having had schooling can result in better physical outcomes for them.

    Sen, Purna. 1999. "Enhancing Women's Choices in Responding to Domestic Violence in Calcutta: A Comparison of Employment and Education." *European Journal of Development Research* 11 (2): 65–86.

    Jejeebhoy, Shireen J. 1998. "Wife-Beating in Rural India: A Husband's Right? Evidence from Survey Data." *Economic and Political Weekly* 23 (15): 855–62.

2. Female Education Can Decrease Female Genital Cutting

The practice of female genital cutting is more common among less-educated women. In addition, research suggests that educated mothers are less likely to subject their daughters to the practice.

- **A Kenyan study found that educated women are four times as likely as uneducated women to oppose female genital cutting.** Women who had some secondary education were four times more likely to oppose female genital cutting both in general and for their daughters and granddaughters as were women who had never completed primary school.

    ORC Macro International Inc. 1995. *Demographic and Health Survey—Kenya.* Calverton, Md.: ORC Macro International Inc.

- **Studies of Egypt have found that mothers' education is associated with lesser intent to circumcise young girls,** lower risks of circumcision, and greater use of medical means of circumcision when girls are circumcised.

Malhotra, Anju, Caren Grown, and Rohini Pande. 2003. "Impact of Investments in Female Education on Gender Inequality." Washington, D.C.: International Center for Research on Women.

- **A Burkina Faso study found that educated women are about 40 percent less likely to have their daughters subjected to female genital cutting.** Some 78 percent of girls whose mothers had not graduated from primary school had been subjected to the practice, compared to 48 percent of girls whose mothers who had received some secondary education.

    World Health Organization. 1998. "Female Genital Mutilation." Geneva: World Health Organization.

- **Several African studies have found that female genital cutting is more prevalent among less-educated women.** According to this report, "those [women] with primary or no education are more likely to have been cut than those who have received secondary level instruction." In the Central African Republic, 48 percent of women with no education and 45 percent with primary education have been cut, while only 23 percent of women with secondary education have been subjected to the practice.

    Population Reference Bureau. 2001. "Abandoning Female Genital Cutting: Prevalence, Attitudes, and Efforts to End the Practice." Washington, D.C.: Population Reference Bureau.

- **An Ivory Coast study found that educated girls were only half as likely to experience female genital cutting.** The study found that fully 55 percent of women with no education had experienced the practice, while among those with a primary education or more the prevalence was only 24 percent.

    World Health Organization. 1998. "Female Genital Mutilation." Geneva: World Health Organization.

3. Educated Women Gain Resources and Influence That Improves Their Own and Their Children's Well-Being

Research from Bangladesh, Brazil, India, and Côte d'Ivoire shows women spend more of whatever income and assets they control on their families as compared with men, who spend relatively more on consumer goods. The more education the women have, the more resources they have, and the stronger their position in the family. Since women tend to spend more on children, the children benefit more from their mothers' education. The result is healthier and better-educated children.

- **In Brazil, women's resources have 20 times the impact on children's health compared with men's resources.** This study found that resources in the hands of women in Brazil affects children's health more than income in the hands of men. For child survival, the marginal impact of female income is almost 20 times as large as that for male income.

Thomas, Duncan. 1990. "Intra-household Allocation: An Inferential Approach." *Journal of Human Resources* 25 (4): 635–64.

- **A study in Côte d'Ivoire found that mothers invest more money in families.** This study found that increasing women's share of cash income in the family increases, on average, the share of the family budget going to food and reduces the share going to alcohol and cigarettes, controlling for income and other factors.

  Hoddinott, John, and Lawrence Haddad. 1995. "Does Female Income Share Influence Household Expenditures? Evidence from Cote d'Ivoire." *Oxford Bulletin of Economics and Statistics* 57 (1): 77–96.

- **A Bangladesh study has found that women's participation in microcredit programs improves children's outcomes more than men's participation does.** In Bangladesh, borrowing by women from Grameen Bank has more positive impact on children's nutritional status and school enrollments than borrowing by men does.

  Khandkher, Shahidur. 1998. *Fighting Poverty with Microcredit: Experience in Rural Bangladesh.* Washington, D.C.: World Bank.

4. Education Can Foster Democracy and Women's Political Participation

The effects of education for men and women on the political process have only recently been studied, but initial findings suggest that education tends to promote more representative, effective government.

- **A 100-country study found that educating girls tends to promote democracy.** A review of data from more than 100 countries found that the emergence of democracy followed increases in primary enrollments, particularly when girls' enrollments caught up to the levels of boys' enrollments. The study argues that these findings confirm the hypothesis that "expanded educational opportunities for females goes along with a social structure that is generally more participatory and, hence, more receptive to democracy."

BOX **5**

Educating Girls May Well Be the Highest-Return Investment

According to Lawrence Summers, "an extensive body of recent research . . . has convinced me that once its benefits are recognized, investment in girls' education may well be the highest return investment available in the developing world. Female deprivation," he argued, "results from a vicious cycle where girls are not educated because they are not expected to make an economic contribution to their families; an expectation that represents a self-fulfilling prophecy. . . . [I]ncreasing educational opportunities for girls offers the best prospect for cutting into this vicious cycle."

"The question," Summers concluded, "is not whether countries can afford this investment, but whether countries can afford not to educate more girls. . . . Expenditures on increasing the education of girls do not just meet the seemingly easy test of being more socially productive than military outlays. They appear to be far more productive than many other valuable categories of investment."

Summers, Lawrence H. 1994. "Investing in All the People: Educating Women in Developing Countries." EDI Seminar Paper No. 45. Washington, D.C.: World Bank.

Barro, Robert J. 1999. "Determinants of Democracy." *Journal of Political Economy* 107 (6): S158–83.

- **Education is linked to more democratic, less corrupt institutions,** a study has found. Recent research has suggested that governments and other institutions function better and with less corruption as women gain education and approach parity with men.

  Basu, Ananya, and Elizabeth M. King. 2001. "Does Education Promote Growth and Democracy? Some Evidence from East Asia and Latin America." Washington, D.C.: World Bank.

- **A Bangladesh study found that educated women are three times as likely to participate in political meetings.** This study found that, while illiterate women would sometimes attend political meetings to listen to the proceedings, educated women were much more likely to attend and participate in the proceedings.

  United Nations Educational, Cultural, and Scientific Organization (UNESCO). 2000. "Women and Girls: Education, Not Discrimination." Paris: UNESCO.

- **Less-educated women discuss political issues less frequently, a 43-country study has shown.** Education makes women more likely to discuss political issues, even controlling for income and other variables.

  Inglehart, Ronald, Miguel Basanez, and Alejandro Moreno. 1998. *Human Values and Beliefs: A Cross-Cultural Sourcebook: Political, Religious, Sexual, and Economic Norms in 43 Societies: Findings from the 1990–1993 World Values Survey.* Ann Arbor: University of Michigan Press.

III. Understanding the Disconnect: The Benefits of Girls' Education versus the Low Levels of Girls' Enrollment and Attainment

A. The "Public Good" Case:
Why Government Intervention Is Essential

If girls' education brings such benefits to girls themselves, their families, and society, why do we not see more girls educated for longer? Where education is not mandatory, the decision to educate children falls to the parents, who incur costs now, yet cannot capture most of the benefits, since they accrue across a child's lifetime and to society as a whole. Parents everywhere care about their children's future, but especially for poor parents, education may seem unaffordable or, if education is of poor quality, unlikely to pay off.

Therefore, a determination based solely on the cost-benefit calculation of parents may lead to a nation's underinvesting in education. The private market, left to itself, will not reach all children and tends particularly to neglect poor girls. Although some parents may be able to afford and access private education for their children, no country in the world has successfully developed without a public education system supported by government.

Developing-country governments need to implement policies that align the cost-benefit calculations of parents with the costs and benefits to their nations as a whole. Mounting evidence suggests that the most effective way for governments to achieve this objective is to make universal education (primary as step one, but also secondary) free and effectively mandatory, while undertaking the investments in reform necessary to improve the quality and benefits of education. Achieving quality universal education may require substantial national and external resources and may, for a number of countries, be beyond immediate reach.

But progress—substantial progress—toward that goal is within reach today. Whether a country is close to achieving high-quality universal basic education or just taking steps in that direction, research and experience show a number of effective ways to better align individual and national cost-benefit calculations. In all of these efforts, improvements in the quality of, as well as access to, education will encourage parents to send children to school and increase the national government's willingness to invest in education.

B. Additional Challenges of Educating Girls

To educate girls, the need for government intervention is even greater, because to parents, the costs may seem higher and the benefits more distant and harder to capture.

- **On the benefit side:** Where sons traditionally help aging parents but daughters "marry out" and join husbands' families, the benefits of educating girls may seem more dubious to parents. One often hears in a variety of country circumstances some form of the expression "why water another man's garden?" Parents who are poor and face budgeting for a dowry for their daughters may consider girls an economic burden to the family. Families may be as extreme as to deliberately neglect daughters to provide for sons. Such "son preference" manifests in parts of Asia and Africa—where girls' enrollments are in fact lowest in absolute terms and compared with boys'.

- **On the cost side:** As basic economics suggests, when the cost of schooling increases for parents, holding quality constant, the amount of education they demand for their children falls. Extensive evidence from many countries shows that the poorer the parents are, the sharper that trade-off is. Many studies show that where son preference is strong, the trade-off tends to be sharper for girls than for boys. The actual costs of schooling may also be higher for girls than for boys. In Tanzania, for instance, parents spend up to 14 percent more to educate a girl, and in Guinea 11 percent. In Uganda and Zambia, according to a cross-country study, spending on girls at the primary level is greater than for boys because the costs for girls are higher.

  Boyle, Siobhan, et al. 2002. "Reaching the Poor: The 'Costs' of Sending Children to School." London: DfID Education Papers series.

- **Four costs to parents of educating girls:**

  1. **Direct Fees.** In many countries, children pay tuition or other fees to attend school. Studies show these fees can amount to 5–10 percent of household income—or 20–30 percent for poorer families. In Uganda, Bangladesh, Zambia, and Nepal, education spending ranked on average as the second or third major household expenditure, in a survey of poor households. The fees may be similar for girls or boys, but parents may be less willing to pay them for girls.

2. **Indirect Fees.** In addition to direct payments for schooling, and even in areas where such payments are not required, there are often indirect fees, such as to parent-teacher associations, charged to parents for having their children attend school. These indirect fees can also include such things as paying for escorts for girls to get to school, supplementing teacher salaries, or finding secure housing for female teachers to stay in rural communities to teach girls.

3. **Indirect Costs: Transport, Clothing, Safety, and Social Criticism.** The costs of transportation and clothing necessary for children to attend school are often significant. These costs may be greater for girls than for boys because families may incur greater clothing expenses for girls to ensure modesty or meet cultural requirements. Girls may also need money for transport to ensure that they are safe and not bothered along the way. In addition, many parents worry that their girls may be subjected to attack or sexual assault once they are at school. In some cultures, just an appearance of impropriety can affect girls' marriage prospects and leave parents concerned about supporting unmarried daughters. Finally, where few girls have ever been educated, parents may be reluctant to be among the first to send girls to school because of the fear of social criticism.

4. **Opportunity Costs: Chore Time and Contribution to Family Income.** In many African and Asian countries, daughters are traditionally expected to do more chores at home than are sons (fetching wood and water or watching siblings, often for several hours daily). In these countries, girls fall victim to a self-fulfilling prophecy. As they are expected to do more, the "opportunity cost" of educating them seems higher and so they are kept home. In some countries, families even rely more on daughters than sons for child wages. In Somalia, for instance, more than half the girls aged 5–14 are working—as well as doing more chores at home.

UNICEF. 2002. "Case Studies on Girls' Education." New York: UNICEF.

Effective government intervention to get girls in school must offset these increased costs for parents and also improve school quality to enhance the benefit side of the equation for both parents and the country as a whole. Where parents already want to educate boys but are on the fence about girls, parents' concerns about cost and quality will matter even more for girls than for boys. Education for girls will have to be of lower cost and better quality to persuade more parents to invest in girls' education.

IV. What Works to Educate Girls: The Evidence

Despite the apparent slow progress in many places, the lack of girls' education is a problem with a known cure. Research over the past decade shows if the costs of education can be kept low and if the quality of education is reasonable, most parents will educate daughters at least at a basic level—even where cultural barriers seem strong. Bangladesh, Brazil, China, Egypt, India, Indonesia, Malawi, Mexico, Oman, Pakistan, Sri Lanka, and Uganda are just some of the countries whose reforms and innovations suggest promising approaches and point to the need for a comprehensive set of policy reforms and programs. In few, if any, cases will any one measure—building latrines, training teachers, or offering scholarships—alone be a "silver bullet." Most evidence suggests that what is needed is a package of policies and programs in four areas:

- **Make girls' schooling more affordable** by eliminating fees and offering targeted scholarships;

- **Provide safe schools nearby,** with at least basic shelter and sanitation and organized to encourage community support, parental involvement, and flexible schedules;

- **Make schools more girl-friendly** by ensuring that schools protect girls' privacy and safety, meet cultural requirements, and actually encourage girls to learn and to look beyond gender stereotypes; and

- **Provide decent quality education,** with enough educated and trained teachers, updated books, and a curriculum that equips girls to cope in the modern world and that parents and girls themselves believe will be useful.

A. Make Girls' Schooling Affordable

The most direct and fastest-acting way for governments to boost school enrollments is to reduce the direct, indirect, and opportunity costs to parents of educating their daughters—by cutting school fees or offering scholarships. Experience suggests that before undertaking such reforms, governments need to prepare for the increases in enrollment that are likely to follow by building schools and training additional teachers. But when governments do, eliminating fees and providing scholarships are critical components of a package of policies to improve access to and quality of education.

1. Reduce Direct Costs: Cutting School Fees Increases Girls' Enrollment

In Malawi, Tanzania, and Uganda, among other countries, dramatic increases in enrollment, especially among girls, soon followed reduction or elimination of school fees. This experience suggests that substantial fees had indeed put poorer children and especially girls at a disadvantage, and cutting fees can help boost enrollments quickly, often dramatically (see Table 1).

- **Enrollment jumped 70 percent after fees were cut and major reforms undertaken in schooling in Uganda,** studies of the reform show. In Uganda, when free schooling was introduced in 1997, primary school enrollment immediately doubled, from 3.4 million to 5.7 million children, and rose to 6.5 million by 1999. Total girls' enrollments went from 63 percent to 83 percent, while enrollment among the poorest fifth of girls went from 46 percent to 82 percent. By 2000, there was virtually no gap between male and female net enrollment ratios

TABLE **1**

Enrollments Surge When Fees Decline

Country	Enrollment during Fees (Millions)	Enrollment after Fee Elimination (Millions)	Percent Growth in Enrollment
Kenya	5.9	7.2	22
Uganda	3.4	6.5	91
Tanzania	1.5	3.0	100
Malawi	1.9	3.1	63

Sources: UNICEF 2003, Bruns et al. 2003.

(89.3 percent versus 88.8 percent), though the gender gap worsened in some areas. By 2003, enrollments climbed again to 7.5 million. (The elimination of fees was part of broader education reforms, so it may not have been responsible for the entire enrollment increase.)

Enrollment increases, however, led to serious problems with crowding and education quality. In response, as part of a broader set of reforms, about 1,000 new teachers are being recruited each month. So far, more than 10,000 teachers have upgraded their qualifications, and the share of untrained teachers in the classrooms has declined by 10 percent. Significant challenges remain, but the reform process has yielded notable progress.

Deininger, Klaus. 2003. "Does Cost of Schooling Affect Enrollment by the Poor? Universal Primary Education in Uganda." *Economics of Education Review* 22 (3): 291–305.

Tomasevski, Katarina. 2003. *Education Denied: Costs and Remedies.* New York: Zed Books.

- **Malawi's efforts to reduce fees and costs helped boost enrollments 63 percent.** When Malawi abolished fees for primary school and made uniforms optional in 1994, enrollments of both boys and girls shot up from 1.9 million to 3.1 million students, an increase of more than 63 percent. By 1996, more than 91 percent of both boys and girls aged 6–11 enrolled in school, compared with just over 50 percent in 1992 (the gender gap then was minimal and actually favored girls).

  While the increase in enrollment was a success, the Malawi case also illustrates the importance of advance planning and resources to support fee reductions. The increase in enrollments nearly overwhelmed Malawi's education system, significantly increasing class size and increasing concerns about education quality. Moreover, "free school" was seen as part of a new move toward democratization, and parents began to regard education as a government responsibility, weakening traditional parental participation.

  Rugh, Andrea. 2000. "Starting Now: Strategies for Helping Girls Complete Primary." SAGE Project. Washington, D.C.: Academy for Educational Development.

BOX **6**

School Fees Burden Poor Families

In the Democratic Republic of Congo, school fees range from $50 to $175 annually per child, but per capita income is only $75. In Mali, Namibia, and Sudan—among the world's poorest countries—school fees are also substantial. Although schooling in Egypt is supposedly free, parents pay fees for uniforms, books, supplies, "additional services," and, above all, tutoring. By 1995, urban parents in Egypt spent about 15 percent of their income on education and rural parents about half that much. In Pakistan, poor families use 8–10 percent of monthly expenditures for education, somewhat less for girls than for boys.

UNICEF. 2002. "Case Studies on Girls' Education." New York: UNICEF.

Rugh, Andrea. 2000. "Starting Now: Strategies for Helping Girls Complete Primary." SAGE Project. Washington, D.C.: Academy for Educational Development.

World Bank. 1996. "Improving Basic Education in Pakistan." Report 14960-PAK. Washington, D.C.: World Bank.

Filmer, Deon. 1999. "The Structure of Social Disparities in Education: Gender and Wealth." Policy Research Report on Gender and Development, Working Paper Series No. 5, World Bank Development Research Group/Poverty and Human Resources. Washington, D.C.: World Bank. May.

- **Attendance doubled in Tanzania after the elimination of fees.** Tanzania eliminated fees for primary school in January 2002, and initial estimates are that 1.5 million additional students, primarily girls, began attending primary school almost immediately. This success has also raised critical issues related to crowding and education quality, as Tanzania now faces the challenge of building and staffing 46,000 new classrooms to cope with the expected 3 million children who will enter the system.

Bruns, Barbara, Alain Mingat, and Ramahatra Rakotomalala. 2003. "Achieving Universal Primary Education by 2015: A Chance for Every Child." Washington, D.C.: World Bank.

Coalition for Health and Education Rights. 2002. "User Fees: The Right to Education and Health Denied." Policy Brief. New York: Coalition for Health and Education Rights.

- **Kenyan experience in the 1970s and 1980s shows that informal school fees discourage enrollment.** After tuition-free education was begun in Kenya in 1974, enrollments in first grade increased 145 percent for boys and 161 percent for girls. But communities were then allowed to introduce other school fees that quadrupled the cost of education in some districts, leading to higher dropout rates. In some districts, research showed that about 40 percent of dropouts were due to high school fees.

Herz, Barbara, et al. 1991. "Letting Girls Learn: Promising Approaches in Primary and Secondary Education." World Bank Discussion Paper No. 133. Washington, D.C.: World Bank.

- **Kenya's new president, Mwai Kibaki, cut fees for primary school, and enrollments soared.** After defeating Daniel Arap Moi in a closely watched election in December 2002, Kibaki fulfilled his promise to remove fees for primary school. Primary school enrollments in Kenya had fallen 10 percent over the 1990s when the school fees were in place. Since fees were eliminated in January 2003, 1.3 million students have entered the school system, for a total of 7.2 million students. As in other countries, the influx of students has created formidable challenges. Classrooms are so crowded that administrators are deferring students' admission. Trained teachers are still scarce, and another 1.5 million children are still out of school.

Lacey, Mark. 2003. "Primary Schools in Kenya, Fees Abolished, Are Filled to Overflowing." *New York Times.* January 7, A8.

UNICEF. 2003. *State of the World's Children 2004.* New York: UNICEF.

- **Asian countries saw enrollments rise after fees were reduced.** A number of Asian countries, including China, Korea, and Sri Lanka, reduced school fees.

The fee reductions were in conjunction with strong government advocacy of education for girls as well as for boys, awareness campaigns, and other efforts to promote girls' education. Sometimes these governments have exempted girls but not boys from the fees, and sometimes just poor girls. Rigorous evaluations of these measures are not available, but enrollment rates for girls as well as boys have risen in these countries and compare well with those of countries of similar income levels.

> Herz, Barbara, et al. 1991. "Letting Girls Learn: Promising Approaches in Primary and Secondary Education." World Bank Discussion Paper No. 133. Washington, D.C.: World Bank.

2. Cover Direct and Indirect Costs and Compensate for Opportunity Costs: Scholarships and Stipends

Increasingly, countries are implementing programs that not only reduce the direct cost of schooling but also help cover the indirect and opportunity costs incurred when parents let children go to school. Since many parents find the costs higher for girls, because of practical concerns about girls' safety as well as lost chore time, scholarships have proved particularly important for girls in such varied settings as Bangladesh, Kenya, and Mexico. Several rigorous studies, including a large controlled experiment in Mexico, have confirmed the strong impact of scholarships on girls' enrollments. Research also suggests that programs that reduce the cost of schooling by providing supplies such as textbooks and uniforms or programs that offer meals or school-based health care can have significant impacts, especially for girls.

- **Secondary school stipends offered through Bangladesh's program lifted girls' enrollment to almost double the national average.** The largest and best-known scholarship program for girls in low-income countries is Bangladesh's national program for stipends for girls in secondary school in rural areas. The program began in 1982 in conjunction with the Bangladesh Rural Action Committee (BRAC) and was first scaled up by the national government to cover one-fourth of all administrative districts. During the first five years that the program ran in pilot areas, girls' enrollments rose from 27 percent to 44 percent, almost double the national average. Under popular pressure, in 1992 the Bangladesh government eliminated girls' tuition and extended the stipend program to all rural areas nationwide. Girls' and boys' enrollments climbed to 55–60 percent, but girls' enrollment climbed faster than boys'.

  - ◆ *How it works:* The stipends cover full tuition and exam costs, textbooks, school supplies, uniforms, transport, and kerosene for lamps. Any girl in grades 6–10 is eligible for the stipends in all 460 rural counties (*thanas*) across Bangladesh as long as she meets three basic criteria: (1) she attends school regularly, (2) she achieves certain minimum grades, and (3) she does not marry while she is in school. She receives the stipend through a bank account in her name.

World Bank. 2001. *Engendering Development.* World Bank Policy Research Report. Washington, D.C., and Oxford: World Bank and Oxford University Press.

Khandkher, S., and Mark Pitt. 2003. "Subsidy to Promote Girls' Secondary Education: The Female Stipend Program in Bangladesh." Washington, D.C.: World Bank.

- **The Bangladeshi scholarship program also encouraged more girls to sit for exams and go to intermediate colleges.** The stipend program's costs are substantial, but the government has found the impact on girls' enrollment and attainment (as well as delayed marriage) impressive enough to continue it on a national scale. The government has expanded the existing program to offer all female students free tuition to both the secondary and the "higher secondary" level.

Rahman, M. Saifur. 2002. "The State of the Economy and the Economic Stabilisation Programme." Speech delivered at Bangladesh Development Forum Meeting, Paris. March 13–15. Available at http://www.gobfinance.org/finance_minister/speech_minister.html.

Khandkher, S., and Mark Pitt. 2003. "Subsidy to Promote Girls' Secondary Education: The Female Stipend Program in Bangladesh." Washington, D.C.: World Bank.

- **The Mexican PROGRESA scholarship program increased across-the-board enrollment and has been successfully scaled up and replicated.** A rigorous randomized evaluation found that nearly all eligible families took advantage of the program, increasing average enrollment by 3.4 percent for all students in grades 1–8. Girls' enrollments improved, especially for children finishing primary school and entering secondary school. The most significant increase (15 percent) was for girls completing grade 6. In part because randomized evaluation of the PROGRESA program allowed for such clear documentation of the program's positive impacts, the program was expanded within Mexico and by 2000 reached 2.6 million families, or 10 percent of the families in Mexico. (The program's budget was also substantial, at $800 million, or 0.2 percent of gross domestic product.)

  - *How it works:* Families receive monthly payments for each child in school, which increase with the age of the child, from about $7 through the third year of primary school to about $25 through the third year of secondary school—contingent on children maintaining 85 percent attendance. Participants also received free health-care services, contingent on regular attendance at clinics and educational sessions.

  - The program has now expanded to urban areas and is called Oportunidades.

Schultz, T. Paul. Forthcoming. "School Subsidies for the Poor: Evaluating the Mexican PROGRESA Poverty Program." *Journal of Development Economics.*

Morley, Steven, and David Coady. 2003. *From Social Assistance to Social Development: Targeted Education Subsidies in Developing Countries.* Washington, D.C.: Center for Global Development/IFPRI.

- **Brazil's Bolsa Escola stipend program virtually eliminated dropouts.** Preliminary evaluations suggest the program will help enroll one-third of all out-of-school children ages 10–15. Program evaluations have found over the first years of the program that none of the girls whose families were enrolled dropped out of school. Although it is too early to have comprehensive data on the national program, models based on household surveys and pilot responses find that about one-third of all unenrolled 10- to 15-year-olds will enroll in response to the program. Among poor households this proportion rises to 50 percent.

  - ◆ *How it works:* A scholarship is paid per family rather than per child. The average monthly transfer is $40 per family, and 90 percent attendance for all children is required. In addition, all children enrolled in Bolsa Escola receive a savings account, into which a small contribution is made every time they are promoted to a higher grade.

    > Government of the Federal District of Brazil. 1997. Department of Education (SE), Executive Secretariat for the Bolsa-Escola Program. Cited in Silvio Caccia Bava, "Bolsa-Escola (School Bursary Program): A Public Policy on Minimum Income and Education." IDRC Policy Brief.

    > Morley, Steven, and David Coady. 2003. *From Social Assistance to Social Development: Targeted Education Subsidies in Developing Countries.* Washington, D.C.: Center for Global Development/IFPRI.

- **A Kenyan program providing free uniforms, textbooks, and classroom construction increased years of schooling attained by 15 percent.** In some areas of Kenya, parents are normally required to purchase school uniforms at a cost of $6 (a significant expense in a country with an average annual per capita income of $340). A rigorous randomized evaluation of a small program that provided free uniforms, textbooks, and classroom construction to 7 of 14 poorly performing schools found that after 5 years, students participating in the program had completed 15 percent more schooling as compared to students in control schools.

  > Kremer, Michael, Sylvie Moulin, and Robert Namunyu. 2002. "Unbalanced Decentralization: Results of a Randomized School Supplies Provision Program in Kenya." Cambridge: Harvard University.

- **The Kenyan girls' scholarship program increased girls' enrollments and test scores.** A girls' scholarship program was introduced at the primary level in 2001, providing two-year merit-based scholarships to girls in two districts in western Kenya on the basis of standardized test scores. Girls eligible for the scholarship had significantly higher test scores and school attendance rates, and test-score improvements persisted even when the girls were no longer eligible to compete for the scholarships. Schools where girls were eligible for the scholarships also saw significant increases in teacher attendance.

Kremer, Michael, Edward Miguel, and Rebecca Thornton. 2003. "Interim Report on a Randomized Evaluation of the Girls' Scholarship Program." Cambridge: Harvard University.

- **Colombia improved enrollments in secondary education through vouchers.**
  Colombia launched a national education voucher program in 1992 to promote continuation from primary to secondary school. Since government schools were overcrowded but excess capacity existed in private schools, the government ran a lottery to award and fund vouchers for parents to send their kids to private schools. A randomized evaluation found voucher lottery winners were 15–20 percent more likely to attend private school, 10 percent more likely to complete eighth grade, and scored the equivalent of a full grade level higher (0.2 standard deviations) on standardized tests compared to students in the control group. The costs of the program were similar to the costs of providing places in public schools.

King, Elizabeth M., Peter Orazem, and Darin Wohlgemuth. 1999. "Central Mandates and Local Incentives: The Colombia Education Voucher Program." *World Bank Economic Review* 13 (3): 467–91.

Angrist, Joshua, et al. 2002. "Vouchers for Private Schooling in Colombia: Evidence from a Randomized Natural Experiment." *American Economic Review* 92 (5): 1535–58.

- **A Nicaraguan study found that scholarships raise enrollments as much as 30 percentage points.** A study of the Nicaraguan Red de Protección Social (RPS) school scholarship program found that enrollment rates went from an average of 66 percent to 91 percent in RPS communities. In the poorest communities, where initial enrollment rates were slightly lower, enrollments rose by 30 percentage points.

Morley, Steven, and David Coady. 2003. *From Social Assistance to Social Development: Targeted Education Subsidies in Developing Countries.* Washington, D.C.: Center for Global Development/IFPRI.

- **A small fellowship program in Quetta, Pakistan, has boosted girls' enrollments.**
  In randomly chosen poor areas lacking government schools, this program began in 1995 by offering $3 per month to subsidize education for each girl enrolled in a new primary school. Girls' enrollments rose by about one-third. Most new students were girls who had not attended school before. Over 1995–98, despite economic and political upheaval, the program grew from 11 schools with about 2,000 students to 40 schools with 10,000 students. In 1999, all schools remained open. Enrollment rates reached 62 percent for boys and 29 percent for girls.

Kim, Jooseop, Harold Alderman, and Peter Orazem, 1999. "Can Private School Subsidies Increase Enrollment for the Poor? The Quetta Urban Fellowship Program." *World Bank Economic Review* 13 (3): 443–65.

• **One study suggests children in Africa contribute 11–36 percent of the value of family income, so equivalent scholarships could both boost enrollment and immediately ease poverty.** In 2001, the International Labour Organization in coordination with the United Nations Conference on Trade and Development (UNCTAD) conducted a comprehensive simulation of implementing scholarship programs in African countries, based on results from the Brazilian and Mexican experiences. The study found that the value of child labor in rural communities in many African countries can be as much as 35 percent of family incomes. As a result, targeted scholarships to cover the opportunity cost to parents would be one of the most effective ways to achieve the goals of poverty reduction and increased girls' enrollment. The study recommended pilot programs in African countries, tailored to specific country needs, including large rural populations and high incidences of HIV/AIDS.

> International Labour Organization. 2001. "The Minimum Income for School Attendance Initiative." Geneva: Joint ILO/UNCTAD Advisory Group.

3. School-Based Health and Nutrition Programs Also Cover Indirect Costs and Increase Attendance

Poor health may limit school participation. For example, intestinal worms affect a quarter of the world's population and in some developing countries are prevalent among school-age children. Studies suggest that school health programs may be a cost effective way of increasing school participation where many children suffer from poor health.

• **Kenya:** A randomized evaluation of a program that provided twice-yearly school-based mass treatment with inexpensive deworming drugs found health and school attendance rates increased not only among students who were provided with the drugs, but also among students at nearby schools, apparently due to reduced disease transmission. Including this "spillover effect" to children at neighboring schools, the program increased schooling by 0.15 years per person treated at a cost of only $3.50 per additional year of schooling induced.

> Miguel, Edward, and Michael Kremer. 2004. "Worms: Identifying Impacts on Education and Health in the Presence of Treatment Externalities." *Econometrica* 72 (1): 159–217.

• **India:** A randomized evaluation of a school-based health program that provided deworming drugs as well as iron supplementation to a network of preschools in urban India found that after one year, children registered large weight gains, a nearly 50 percent reduction in moderate-to-severe cases of anemia, and a reduction in school absence rates among children ages 4–6.

> Bobonis, Gustavo, Edward Miguel, and Charu Sharma. 2002. "Iron Supplementation and Early Childhood Development: A Randomized Evaluation in India." Berkeley: University of California.

- **School meals in Kenya increase school attendance by 30 percent and boost test scores.** Providing meals for children who attend is another way to help parents afford to send children to school. A randomized evaluation of a small preschool feeding program in Kenya found the meals increased both school attendance and test scores. The evaluation found attendance was 30 percent higher in 25 schools that offered a free breakfast as compared to 25 control schools. Moreover, even though feeding cut into instruction time, as long as the teachers were well trained, test scores still rose by 0.4 standard deviations as compared to scores in control schools.

    Vermeersch, Christel. 2002. "School Meals, Educational Achievement, and School Competition: Evidence from a Randomized Experiment." Cambridge: Harvard University.

- **The U.S. Global Food for Education (FFE) pilot initiative helped increase enrollment by 10 percent or more.** The school feeding initiative focused particularly on supporting programs that targeted girls and others of the most marginalized groups. It has provided meals to 7 million children in 38 countries since 2001. An evaluation in February 2003 found that World Food Programme projects supported through the initiative saw average enrollments increase by 10 percent and girls' enrollments increase by 11.7 percent. Private voluntary organizations that received support reported a 5.75 percent increase in enrollment. Some projects saw enrollment increases as high as 32 percent. The pilot FFE initiative of 2000 was transformed into a permanent program in 2002 and renamed the McGovern-Dole International Food for Education and Child Nutrition Program.

    U.S. Foreign Agriculture Service. 2003. *The Global Food for Education Pilot Program: A Review of Project Implementation and Impact.* Report to the U.S. Congress. February.

- **Combining school feeding programs with take-home rations increased girls' enrollment by about 50 percent.** Programs in a number of countries have targeted girls' enrollment by providing not only in-school feeding programs but also small take-home rations for all girls that attend school. This was intended to assure that children who receive meals at school do not receive less food at home than other siblings. Case studies from four countries—Cameroon, Morocco, Niger, and Pakistan—undertaken by the World Food Program indicate that in each case, girls' attendance increased by at least 50 percent. These studies suggest these increases will last.

    World Food Programme. 2001. "School Feeding Works for Girls' Education." WFP Report. Rome: World Food Programme.

B. Build Local Schools with Community Support and Flexible Schedules

Removing fees or offering scholarships provides little help where children have no schools to attend. Research and program experience suggest that building decent schools nearby and providing trained teachers, teaching materials, and a reasonable curriculum are often enough to bring most boys or girls into school—at least at the primary level and where parents are not desperately poor or traditions do not severely restrict girls and women. Evidence particularly from South Asia and Africa—including areas where hardly any girls have attended school—shows community-based approaches can sharply boost girls' enrollment and achievement in just a few years.

Successful approaches include explicit agreements within the community to educate girls as well as boys, community influence over teacher selection and school operations, and genuine partnerships between communities and the federal government. Often, local nongovernmental organizations (NGOs) help organize such community participation, and parent teacher association (PTA)–type organizations at schools may be established. In addition, community schools that offer flexible schedules or provide child-care support may be particularly successful at increasing girls' enrollment. Research suggests that in many countries, such community-based approaches that are not fees by another name can effectively encourage education, particularly for girls.

1. Building Schools Close to Girls' Homes Boosts Enrollments

Common sense suggests distance matters for any child, but it seems to matter particularly for girls. The farther girls have to walk or travel, the greater their parents'— and their own—concerns for actual safety and for reputation. Research in such diverse countries as Ghana, India, Malaysia, Peru, and Pakistan shows distance matters for all children, and often especially for girls. In parts of Asia and Africa, girls are simply not allowed to attend distant schools.

- **Several studies show distance to school discourages girls' attendance more than it does boys'.** In India, a girl's probability of ever enrolling in school drops by 1–2 percentage points if the distance to primary school increases marginally. In Malaysia, the lack of a secondary school in the community lowers the probability of a girl attending by 17 percentage points.

    Sipahimanlani, Vandana. 1999. "Education in the Rural Indian Household: The Impact of Household and School Characteristics on Gender Differences." Working Paper 68. New Delhi: National Council of Applied Economic Research.

    Lavy, Victor. 1996. "School Supply Constraints and Children's Educational Outcomes in Rural Ghana." *Journal of Development Economics* 51 (2): 291–314.

Gertler, Paul, and Paul Glewwe. 1992. "The Willingness to Pay for Education for Daughters in Contrast to Sons: Evidence from Rural Peru." *World Bank Economic Review* 6 (1): 171–88.

King, Elizabeth M., and Lee A. Lillard. 1987. "Education Policy and Schooling Attainment in Malaysia and the Philippines." *Economics of Education Review* 6 (2): 167–81.

- **Indonesia achieved nearly full enrollment by building and staffing conveniently located schools.** An in-depth analysis of Indonesia's education reform program shows the importance of providing a decent school nearby. Indonesia built more than 60,000 new schools over four years, making schools convenient for more children to reach. Critically, however, the government did not just supply a building; it made sure schools had enough trained teachers, books, and learning materials. A study found that each new school built increased the average attendance by 0.24 to 0.38 school years for the first generation of children to enter school. Indonesia has maintained over 90 percent primary enrollment for both girls and boys since the reforms (see Appendix).

  Duflo, Esther. 2001. "Schooling and Labor Market Consequences of School Construction in Indonesia: Evidence from an Unusual Policy Experiment." *American Economic Review* 91 (4): 795–813.

- **An Egyptian study found that new schools boost rural girls' enrollments 60 percent.** In the 1980s and 1990s, Egypt constructed some 2,000 new schools and provided teachers in them. Girls' enrollments in rural primary schools increased about 60 percent, from 897,000 in 1981–82 to 1.4 million in 1990–91. The gender gap decreased significantly: the proportion of female students rose from 35 percent to 42 percent of total enrollments in rural primary schools. Comparing trends in the new-school locales to the broader regional data, enrollment in the new-school areas grew by 18 percent more than enrollment in the broader area. Girls' enrollments grew by 23 percent.

  Rugh, Andrea. 2000. "Starting Now: Strategies for Helping Girls Complete Primary." SAGE Project. Washington, D.C.: Academy for Educational Development.

- **A cross-country study has found that school-aged children are 10–20 percentage points more likely to attend school if they live in a village with a primary school.** A World Bank study found that having any school present in a rural village boosts enrollment of children aged 6–14 in the nine countries studied. The presence of a secondary school also boosted enrollments in several countries. The presence of a school affects girls' enrollments differently in different countries: it has a larger effect on girls than on boys in Benin, India, and Zimbabwe, but that pattern is not universal.

  Filmer, Deon. 1999. "The Structure of Social Disparities in Education: Gender and Wealth." Policy Research Report on Gender and Development, Working Paper Series No. 5, World Bank Development Research Group/Poverty and Human Resources. Washington, D.C.: World Bank. May.

2. Community Involvement in Local Schools Can Be Key

Small schools close to home may also increase parental involvement and attract more students, especially girls. Promising strategies are emerging, especially in Africa and South Asia, which include local recruitment of teachers, more interactive teaching methods, and greater community involvement in school operations (often in PTA-type arrangements). Although community-based approaches offer great promise, there are also risks. The government may feel "off the hook" if communities try to shoulder the main burden of schooling children; communities may lack the resources to do the job; issues of curriculum content may arise; and tensions may build between government, NGOs, and communities. Finding ways to address these risks and to both increase community participation and strengthen the public education system is key to forging a credible compact between parents, teachers, NGOs, and government.

- **In Pakistan's Balochistan province, parental involvement in government schools permitted "genderless" schools that boosted girls' enrollments 30 percent. Community-based approaches in more remote areas achieved even more.** In 1990, Balochistan had 11 times as many boys' as girls' schools, and girls' enrollments were about 14 percent (compared to roughly 30 percent for Pakistan as a whole). As education policy was discussed and new government schools were built, parents agreed to let younger girls and boys attend "genderless" schools. By 1994, girls' enrollments in Balochistan climbed by almost one-third, to 18 percent. In extremely remote areas lacking government schools, community schools were organized in 1993. By November 1994, 198 community schools had been set up and 10,000 girls were enrolled—an astonishing 87 percent of girls enrolled in community schools compared with the provincial average of 18 percent.

  World Bank. 1996. "Improving Basic Education in Pakistan." Report 14960-PAK. Washington, D.C.: World Bank.

- **The Bangladesh Rural Action Committee (BRAC) pioneered a highly successful, nonformal, community-based school approach to reach the most needy kids and help them transition into the public system.** The community school approach has achieved nearly double the completion rates of government schools (90 percent versus 53 percent in a 1990 study) and has proven highly effective at transferring students from the nonformal base into the formal system—at a rate of 78 percent according to a 1993 study. A comprehensive assessment of BRAC's community school program concludes that "[BRAC] unquestionably leads to the increased participation of children in terms of enrollment, attendance, and completion."

  Rugh, Andrea, and Heather Bossert. 1998. *Involving Communities: Participation in the Delivery of Education Programs.* Washington, D.C.: Creative Associates International, ABEL Project Consortium, USAID.

• **Colombia's "Escuela Nueva" program of multigrade community schools contributed to a 30 percent increase in rural enrollment.** Escuela Nueva was implemented in 1975 by Colombia's Education Ministry, as a way to target rural areas, which, as in many countries, lagged far behind urban areas in terms of educational attainment. The program established Escuela Nueva schools in poor rural communities where students of different ages, grades, and abilities were taught in the same classroom and were provided more flexible schedules. Because of the challenge of teaching such a variety of students, teachers were trained in active-learning techniques and encouraged to break from the rote methods taught in conventional schools. In contrast to BRAC, Escuela Nueva provided an alternative within (rather than outside) the formal education system.

The piloting process was slow and difficult, and the program faced strong initial resistance. But Escuela Nueva was eventually brought to scale in the late 1980s in 18,000 classrooms. A study in 1992 found that rural enrollment increased from about 50 percent to 80 percent, with girls attending Escuela Nueva schools more frequently than boys. In 1994, the Escuela Nueva approach was implemented in poor areas of Cali and Bogota and has been replicated in a number of other Latin American countries. A more recent study has found that teacher innovation is a strong component of the success of the community-based multigrade school approach, and that Escuela Nueva in Colombia is an example of "one of the most successful multi-grade schooling programs."

> Benveniste, L., and P. J. McEwan. 2000. "Constraints to Implementing Educational Innovations: The Case of Multi-Grade Schools." *International Review of Education* 46 (1–2): 31–48.

> Rugh, Andrea, and Heather Bossert. 1998. *Involving Communities: Participation in the Delivery of Education Programs.* Washington, D.C.: Creative Associates International, ABEL Project Consortium, USAID.

• **A 16-country review in Africa shows that community schools generally increase enrollment, retention, and quality, and on average have lower dropout rates.** Despite differences in approach (new construction versus support of existing schools; varying levels of government versus NGO involvement), the study found broadly consistent trends. For example, World Learning in Ethiopia has seen girls' enrollment increase by 13.8 percent; the Community School Alliances project in Ghana reports that nearly every child in participating communities was enrolled by the end of the project; girls' enrollment in southern Sudan increased 96 percent as a result of the work of community education committees sensitizing parents and the community on the need to educate girls; and in Malawi, children in community-based schools score 30 percent higher than children in government schools on national tests.

> Miller-Grandvaux, Yolande, and Karla Yoder. 2002. "A Literature Review of Community Schools in Africa." Washington, D.C.: U.S. Agency for International Development (USAID) Bureau for Africa.

- **Community schools in Mali have raised girls' enrollments by 67 percent.** Mali's efforts to promote community participation to encourage girls' education are among the best known in Africa. Between 1989 and 1993, a program to encourage and support local community schools increased overall girls' enrollment by 67 percent and increased by 83 percent the number of 7-year-old girls entering primary school. As of 2000, 1,500 community schools were operating, serving about 8 percent of Mali's schoolchildren. Communities are now building more locally accessible schools and involving communities in the design and operation of the schools so that they meet cultural norms. The program is also setting quotas for both boys and girls, developing more relevant "life skills" in the curriculum, and using local languages in instruction. Rigorous research is not available on the impact of more recent programs, but early indications are that girls' enrollments and test scores are increasing.

  > Rugh, Andrea. 2000. "Starting Now: Strategies for Helping Girls Complete Primary." SAGE Project. Washington, D.C.: Academy for Educational Development.

  > Tietjen, Karen. 1999. "Community Schools in Mali: A Comparative Cost Study." SD Publication Series Technical Paper No. 97. Washington, D.C.: Health and Human Resources Analysis for Africa Project, USAID.

- **A community remedial education program in India has dramatically improved learning.** A recent randomized study evaluated a community-based remedial education program in India that was run in two separate cities (Mumbai and Vadodara) and has involved over 15,000 students. The remedial education program hires young women from the community to teach basic literacy and numeracy skills to children who don't have basic skills by the third grade. The evaluation found that after two years the remedial education program increased learning by 0.39 standard deviations, with the highest gains among the least able students (a result notable for educational programs in developing countries). Moreover, because the program hires local high-school-educated girls to teach classes of around 20 students, the average cost of the program is only $5 per child per year. At the margin, extending this program could be 12–16 times more cost effective than hiring new teachers.

  > Banerjee, Abhijit, et al. 2003. "Remedying Education: Evidence from Two Randomized Experiments in India." Cambridge: Massachusetts Institute of Technology.

- **A study has found that community schools in Mali are 14 percent less expensive than regular schools.** A number of studies and field practitioners have found that community schools are less expensive to set up and run than more traditional, centralized schools. One study in Mali found it cost $36 per year to educate a student at a community school compared to $42 per year at the regular district school. Practitioners have found similar results in comparable countries.

  > Tietjen, Karen. 1999. "Community Schools in Mali: A Comparative Cost Study." SD Publication Series Technical Paper No. 97. Washington, D.C.: Health and Human Resources Analysis for Africa Project, USAID.

BOX **7**

Innovation in Community Approaches

Although rigorous academic reviews of them are not yet available, many new community approaches are seen as highly promising by practitioners and experts in the field. Some of these programs are championed by the Forum for African Women Educationalists (FAWE):

Parental Advisory Committees (PACs) in Ethiopia. In certain areas in Egypt, local parental advisory committees are taking responsibility for important community issues related to girls' schooling. Members of the PACs meet directly with parents of teenage girls to discourage early marriage and encourage enrolling their girls in school. These committees also meet with men who have indicated a desire to marry young girls in the community to discourage such behavior. There are cases of these committees' helping to track down and recover girls who were abducted from their families.

Ethiopian Ministry of Education. 2002. "Education Sector Development Program: 2002/03–2004/05." Addis Ababa. May.

Sperling, Gene. 2002. Interview with Ethiopian Education Minister Genet Zewde and PAC members. Ethiopia. April.

Mothers Clubs in Gambia. In collaboration with UNICEF and FAWE-Gambia, mothers clubs have been established in more than 40 communities in Gambia. Mothers who send their girls to school get to join these clubs, which provide income-generating assistance, including small business workshops and skill development (tie and dying, knitting, soap making, pottery, etc.). The clubs generate considerable excitement as well as increase mothers' skills, and they seem, based on preliminary assessments, to increase girls' enrollment.

Ndong-Jatta, Ann Therese. 2002. "Providing Quality Basic Education for All: A New Focus." Presentation by Gambian Secretary of Education. June 11.

Girls Clubs in Ghana. In partnership with FAWE-Ghana, local communities have established after-school clubs for girls only. These clubs provide health and rights education for girls and put on plays and other arts demonstrations promoting respect for girls and women, encouraging girls to stay in school. Initial results from the program are strongly positive: it has increased achievement

---

3. Providing Flexible Schedules and Services Can Help Enroll Girls

In general, offering flexible schedules in both regular and informal schools helps boost enrollments by accommodating children's work—making it easier for children to care for younger siblings, do chores, or even work for wages while enrolled in school. These options have been most effectively implemented in community school settings where it is easier for the community to support and sustain flexible approaches. Such efforts do pose a dilemma: they make it easier for children to attend but may make it harder for them to spend time studying. Yet for many poor children it may be the most realistic option for receiving an education. Ultimately, it is important to help children gain time to go to school and to study and, where children are in informal schools, to enable them to make the transition to regular schools.

BOX 7 (continued)

among the girls who attend the clubs and reduced dropout rates among all girls at the schools where the program operates.

Churcher, Christine. 2002. "Models for Promoting EFA: What's Working, What's Not?" Presentation to Conference at Center for Universal Education. Washington, D.C. June 11.

Ethiopia's Basic Education Systematic Overhaul. Under a new partnership with USAID and local NGOs, the Ethiopian Education Ministry is implementing a program of community action projects whereby communities commit to education planning every step of the way and receive resources to implement their visions. Community groups are expected to identify needs and develop guidelines for reform or rebuilding of local school facilities. They must also raise 5–10 percent of the cost of government expenditures on these projects. The money is not raised from fees, however; instead, it is raised by the community, often by engaging wealthy members of the community or even alumni of the school. Once funds are raised,

the community takes primary responsibility for overseeing the project. Among many other improvements, the program has led to the creation or renovation of 4,225 classrooms and 32,659 new desks.

Sperling, Gene. 2002. "Ethiopia Provides Glimpse of Hope for Its Future." *Bloomberg.* April 15.

Ethiopian Ministry of Education. 2002. "Education Sector Development Program: 2002/03–2004/05." Addis Ababa. May.

Rural Teacher Assistance in Gambia. To address the critical issue of teacher shortages (especially of female teachers) in rural areas, the Gambian government is experimenting with different incentives, such as building new housing in remote areas and establishing a "Teacher Housing Loan Scheme" to help teachers afford decent accommodations.

Ndong-Jatta, Ann Therese. 2002. "Providing Quality Basic Education for All: A New Focus." Presentation by Gambian Secretary of Education. June 11.

- Many countries are trying flexible school hours to help boost girls' enrollments. In both formal and informal school settings, flexible hours have been employed to make it easier on children, and especially girls, to attend. For example, in India, efforts to provide flexible hours through nonformal education helped draw working children, especially girls, into primary school. Colombia's Escuela Nueva program includes flexible schedules for different grades. Part-time and flexible scheduling also helped raise girls' enrollments in China.

> Herz, Barbara, et al. 1991. "Letting Girls Learn: Promising Approaches in Primary and Secondary Education." World Bank Discussion Paper No. 133. Washington, D.C.: World Bank.

- **A study of Bangladesh's BRAC program finds flexible "satellite" schools raise girls' primary enrollments.** Part of the BRAC model was a "satellite" school experiment, in which two or three small schools covering at least the first three primary grades were established closer to the community and supervised by a more distant main primary school. The satellite schools operated only 2.5 hours daily, mainly with women teachers, and school schedules were set to suit rural children's work. Participation rates were greater than what was expected, girls comprised 63 percent of students enrolled, and fewer than 1 percent dropped out.

Herz, Barbara, et al. 1991. "Letting Girls Learn: Promising Approaches in Primary and Secondary Education." World Bank Discussion Paper No. 133. Washington, D.C.: World Bank.

- **Double sessions in Pakistan's Northern Areas enrolled girls for the first time.** Parents asked government schools to have double sessions, with boys attending until 2 p.m., and girls attending afterward. Such schedules and the hiring of female teachers helped boost girls' enrollments.

World Bank. 1996. "Improving Basic Education in Pakistan." Report 14960-PAK. Washington, D.C.: World Bank.

Herz, Barbara. 2002. "Universal Basic Education: What Works." Paper prepared for the Coalition for Basic Education. Washington, D.C.: Academy for Educational Development.

4. Providing Preschool and Child-Care Programs Appears Promising

Although rigorous evidence is scarce, some studies suggest that providing affordable child care or lowering the cost of community-based child care can help girls who care for their siblings to attend school.

- **A Kenyan study found that a 10 percent jump in child-care costs cut girls' attendance 13 percent.** On the margin, the study found, an increase in mothers' wages raises school enrollments for boys but reduces enrollments for girls, as more mothers can afford to send boys to school but ask daughters to handle household tasks while they are at work. Yet a 10 percent increase in mothers' wages also increases by 3 percent the proportion of households sending all their children to school, as schooling costs become more manageable.

Lokshin, Michael, Elena Glinskaya, and Marito Garcia. 2000. "The Effect of Early Childhood Development Programs on Women's Labor Force Participation and Older Children's Schooling in Kenya." Policy Research Report on Gender and Development Working Paper Series No. 15, World Bank Development Research Group. Washington, D.C.: World Bank.

- **One Indian program has boosted enrollments with village preschools.** One study discusses India's effort to set up centers offering early education classes near or in village primary schools. These were intended to promote early childhood development and to help substitute for the child care that may keep girls from attending primary school. The centers do not accept children younger than two years of age, however, and so toddlers often roam fairly freely in villages.

The study indicates that the centers help introduce poor children from illiterate families to the school environment, and these children tend to continue on into the formal primary school program.

Rugh, Andrea. 2000. "Starting Now: Strategies for Helping Girls Complete Primary." SAGE Project. Washington, D.C.: Academy for Educational Development.

- **A Nepali program in early childhood development and parental training particularly boosts girls' attendance.** Roughly 13,000 children participated in this program. They tend to enroll at higher rates in primary school, have low repetition and high promotion rates, and are less likely to drop out. Enrollment rates for girls and very poor and low-caste children who participated in the program are similar to those for high-caste boys, and they are succeeding, as well. The parents of participating children are also more likely to engage with the children's teachers and schools.

  Save the Children. 2000. "What's the Difference? The Impact of Early Childhood Development Programs." Kathmandu: Save the Children.

C. Make Schools More Girl-Friendly

While having a basic school nearby is an important first step, it may not suffice to bring all girls into school or to keep them there. Research has identified a number of additional—but still basic—measures important for increasing girls' enrollment, for both practical and cultural reasons. It appears that, especially as girls get older, having private latrine facilities in schools is critical, not just nice. More generally, assuring girls' privacy and safety in line with cultural expectations may be essential. In some places, training female teachers who are culturally acceptable to parents is key to increasing girls' enrollment. And teaching in ways that encourage, rather than discourage, girls to look beyond gender stereotypes only makes sense. Many measures to make schools more girl-friendly carry relatively low costs.

1. Private Latrine Facilities Are Essential

- **A Pakistani study found that parents require latrine facilities for girls.** A study in four areas of Pakistan found that if parents are to enroll children, they expect a school will be solidly built with a boundary wall and have a water pump and latrine. The latrine is a necessity.

  World Bank. 1996. "Improving Basic Education in Pakistan." Report 14960-PAK. Washington, D.C.: World Bank.

- **Girls in African countries tend to miss school during menses if no private toilet or latrine is available.** Experience across 30 African countries shows that where no private toilet facilities are available at school, the majority of young women will not attend school during menses because they have no adequate way to take care of personal hygiene. To avoid this problem, girls need access to toilet facilities that are separate from those for boys and not too crowded. It is common in some areas for schools to have only one toilet for every 80 children or more.

FAWE. 2001. "Girls' Education and Poverty Eradication: FAWE's Response." Presentation to the Third United Nations Conference on the Least Developed Countries. Brussels, Belgium. May 10–20.

2. Ensuring Girls' Privacy and Safety in Line with Cultural Requirements Is Key

It is only common sense that parents expect their children to be safe at school. In some cases, however, cultural requirements for privacy must also be respected. These may entail separate schools for girls, separate hours for girls in schools shared with boys, boundary walls for girls' schools, female teachers, and the like. Such efforts are critical not only for increasing enrollments, but for achieving gender parity in primary education. Involving communities has emerged as the best way to find out what matters most to parents and how to proceed.

World Bank. 2001. *Engendering Development.* World Bank Policy Research Report. Washington, D.C., and Oxford: World Bank and Oxford University Press.

Herz, Barbara. 2002. "Universal Basic Education: What Works." Paper prepared for the Coalition for Basic Education. Washington, D.C.: Academy for Educational Development.

3. Teach in Ways That Encourage Girls to Achieve and That Discourage Gender Stereotypes

It can be expensive to change textbooks to reduce gender stereotyping, but it is certainly important that it happen. It is also important to train teachers to discourage gender stereotyping. Although research on the impact of specific programs is scarce, such efforts are under way in a number of countries and should be explored and analyzed more intensively.

- **Studies find that traditional curricula and materials portray women as passive.** A study of one country's curriculum found that 90 percent of the people discussed or illustrated in textbooks were male. A study of another curriculum found that, while males mentioned were often described as leaders, fighters, or soldiers, girls were most often described as breast-feeders, pretty, or pregnant.

Gachukia, E., W. M. Kabira, and M. Masinjila. 1992. "Meeting the Basic Learning Needs of Adolescent Mothers in Kenya: A Situation Analysis." Nairobi: International Childhood Development Centre and UNICEF KCO.

Obura, A. 1985. "The Image of Girls and Women in Primary Textbooks in Kenya." Nairobi: University of Nairobi.

Biraimah, Karen Coffyn. 1980. "Different Knowledge for Different Folks: Knowledge Distribution in a Togolese Secondary School." In Philip G. Altbock, Robert F. Arnove, and Gail P. Kelly, eds., *Comparative Education.* New York: Macmillan.

Ethiopian Ministry of Education. 1980. "Gender Analysis of Primary School Textbooks."

- **Countries are using gender sensitivity training for teachers and administrators to encourage girls to participate.** In Africa, a number of countries including Angola, Benin, Cameroon, Eritrea, and Malawi have tried such teacher training, as have countries elsewhere (see Box 8). Effective approaches include encouraging respect for girls and boys equally, making sure girls can participate in class equally with boys, encouraging girls to study subjects such as math and science where fewer girls than boys have done so, expressing similar expectations for boys and girls in learning performance, and suggesting nontraditional occupations for girls. In some cases, separating girls and boys (either in separate schools or for subjects such as math where girls have been reluctant) has reportedly promoted girls' learning.

> UNICEF. 2001. *Fourth Consolidated Report to the Government of Norway on the UNICEF African Girls' Education Initiative.* New York: UNICEF Program Division/Education Section.
>
> King, Elizabeth M., and M. Anne Hill, eds. 1993. *Women's Education in Developing Countries.* Baltimore: Johns Hopkins University Press.

- **Teachers' attitudes and expectations for girls can influence girls' outcomes.** Whether teachers think math is important for girls and whether boys and girls receive and feel they receive equal treatment in the classroom substantially affects girls' probability of staying in school. Moreover, if teachers think girls are less able, girls tend to underperform, while boys are less affected by teachers' views. In Nigeria, for example, boys are given more opportunities to ask and answer questions, to use learning materials, and to lead groups; girls are given less time on task than boys in science. Such findings would be common in many countries in South Asia as well.

> Lloyd, Cynthia B., Barbara Mensch, and Wesley Clark. 1998. "The Effects of Primary School Quality on the Educational Participation and Attainment of Kenyan Girls and Boys." Population Council Working Paper 116. New York: Population Council.
>
> UNICEF. 2002. "Case Studies on Girls' Education." New York: UNICEF.
>
> UNICEF. 2001. *Fourth Consolidated Report to the Government of Norway on the UNICEF African Girls' Education Initiative.* New York: UNICEF Program Division/Education Section.

BOX **8**

Malawi's Notable Efforts to Address Gender Stereotyping

Along with advocacy of education and measures to cut costs, Malawi has set up a Gender Appropriate Curriculum Unit to improve the curriculum, institute it in schools, and assess results. It has also helped reform teacher training and textbooks. Among African countries, Malawi stands out in its high enrollment rates for both boys and girls in primary and secondary school.

Rugh, Andrea. 2000. "Starting Now: Strategies for Helping Girls Complete Primary." SAGE Project. Washington, D.C.: Academy for Educational Development.

- **Training teachers to combat gender stereotypes improves the learning environment for girls.** Very few teachers are trained in ways of reaching girls effectively or in ways of helping children think beyond gender stereotypes. The result is that girls are often portrayed only in highly restricted roles, teachers themselves expect less of girls, and girls are given less chance to participate and learn.

4. Provide More Female Teachers

Evidence from program evaluations indicates strongly that in certain cultures, or where girls' enrollment rates are relatively low, far more girls will enroll if they can be taught by female teachers, particularly as they approach adolescence. Parents may be concerned that sending girls to school will expose them to physical or sexual abuse from other students or teachers. Others may worry about appearances of impropriety. In some areas, particularly where girls and women are isolated within communities, solving this problem requires hiring more women teachers. However, it can be difficult to find enough qualified women, especially in rural areas where most women have little if any education. Urban women with more education (or their husbands) often will not move to the rural areas to work.

- **Many countries have tried to recruit women teachers with reduced experience or qualifications to work in rural areas to encourage girls' enrollments.** In Mozambique and Botswana, voluntary or interim teachers were hired, with plans to improve recruiting and in-service training for those areas. While community or interim teachers lack sufficient educational qualifications and resources to ensure quality, they are often well situated and eager to teach in their rural areas, especially where teaching is one of the first jobs open to women. Reconciling the demands on teachers with the limited teaching workforce "will be difficult to solve for many countries within the limited budget (and time) frames."

  > Nilsson, Paula. 2003. "Education for All: Teacher Demand and Supply in Africa." Education International Working Paper No. 12. Brussels: Education International. November.

- **In recent years, thousands of qualified women have joined the teaching forces in South Asia and Africa.** Bangladesh, India, and Pakistan have set goals for hiring women teachers, reversing traditional patterns of discrimination. Bangladesh's scholarship program for girls in secondary school could not function without its female teaching force.

  Experience in Africa and the Middle East is similar, particularly where conservative cultural traditions prevail. In all these regions, women teachers provide girls and the community with useful role models. Where few women have worked in the labor force, simply hiring women teachers may encourage families to let girls learn.

World Bank. 2001. *Engendering Development.* World Bank Policy Research Report. Washington, D.C., and Oxford: World Bank and Oxford University Press.

Herz, Barbara, et al. 1991. "Letting Girls Learn: Promising Approaches in Primary and Secondary Education." World Bank Discussion Paper No. 133. Washington, D.C.: World Bank.

Rugh, Andrea. 2000. "Starting Now: Strategies for Helping Girls Complete Primary." SAGE Project. Washington, D.C.: Academy for Educational Development.

Female teachers increase girls' enrollments in informal schools in India. Seva Mandir, an Indian NGO, runs nonformal schools that provide basic numeracy and literacy education to children who do not attend formal school; these schools then attempt to "mainstream" these students into the regular school system. Researchers recently conducted a randomized evaluation of a program that placed a second teacher (where possible, a woman) in classes in these nonformal schools in an attempt to, among other things, improve student learning and make school more attractive to girls. The results of the evaluation showed that girls' attendance increased by about half, although the program did not improve test scores.

Banerjee, Abhijit, Suraj Jacob, and Michael Kremer, with Jenny Lanjouw and Peter Lanjouw. 2000. "Promoting School Participation in Rural Rajasthan: Results from Some Prospective Trials." Cambridge: Harvard University.

Banerjee, Abhijit, and Michael Kremer. 2002. "Teacher-Student Ratios and School Performance in Udaipur, India: A Prospective Evaluation." Cambridge: Harvard University.

BOX **9**

The Need for Women Teachers

Even where girls are not isolated or excluded, having a female teacher can help girls and their parents feel more comfortable. Parents—or girls themselves—may be concerned that girls may be mistreated at school by male teachers or even contract HIV or return home pregnant. Girls, particularly in Africa, seem to face increasing pressure from male teachers: in Cameroon, a recent study reported that teachers had had sexual relationships with 27 percent of the girls surveyed. Some 20 percent of the girls had become pregnant, and of course, many of the girls would also have been exposed to HIV. But hiring female teachers is not just a way to overcome the problems of male teachers; it also offers real advantages. Women teachers may encourage girls more, and they are often inspiring role models, especially where few other women work in the labor force. Recruiting female teachers may not be any more expensive than recruiting men, but finding female teachers, particularly in rural areas where few women are literate, can be difficult. Recruiting voluntary or interim teachers with reduced qualifications may be a temporary solution, but then these teachers may need more training, and women in rural areas also often need safe housing arrangements.

UNICEF. 2003. *State of the World's Children 2004.* New York: UNICEF.

UNICEF. 2002. "Case Studies on Girls' Education." New York: UNICEF.

D. Focus Particularly on Quality of Education

Where parents already want to educate boys but are more ambivalent about girls, improvements in education quality may be particularly important to tip more decisions toward sending girls to school. Although more research is needed on precisely how to improve the quality of education in particular settings, studies find that a first and critical step is to have enough qualified teachers who attend school regularly, and that beyond teachers, schools are more effective at attracting girls if they offer a curriculum that equips children for the twenty-first century and have the requisite books and learning materials.

Curriculum is emerging as a major concern of governments, NGOs, and communities anxious to cope more effectively with such challenges as globalization, HIV/AIDS, environmental pressures, and poverty reduction. Efforts to revamp curricula and improve teaching are core parts of many countries' efforts to expand and improve education, and as they are assessed, knowledge of what works will increase considerably. Children's achievement should be tested regularly to ensure that the quality of education is meeting expectations.

- **An Egyptian study found that low educational quality and lack of learning were the top reasons for dropouts among girls.**

  Rugh, Andrea. 2000. "Starting Now: Strategies for Helping Girls Complete Primary." SAGE Project. Washington, D.C.: Academy for Educational Development.

- **A review of Arab countries found that a focus on rote learning and teaching and a lack of focus on science do not sufficiently prepare students for today's job market or promote critical thinking.**

  UNDP. 2003. *Arab Human Development Report 2003.* New York: UNDP.

- **In Kenya and Bangladesh, research indicates the quality of teaching influences demand for education for girls even more than for boys.**

  Lloyd, Cynthia B., Barbara Mensch, and Wesley Clark. 1998. "The Effects of Primary School Quality on the Educational Participation and Attainment of Kenyan Girls and Boys." Working Paper 116. New York: Population Council.

  Khandkher, Shahidur. 1996. "Education Achievements and School Efficiency in Rural Bangladesh." World Bank Discussion Paper No. 319. Washington, D.C.: World Bank.

1. Provide Enough Teachers

No school can work for boys or girls without a capable, acceptable teacher. Research from poor areas suggests that a good teacher can make a difference in girls' enrollment and attainment even without much of a school building—at least at the primary level.

- **Studies suggest countries should aim for a maximum of 40 students per classroom and must insist that teachers attend more regularly.** Many poor countries, especially in Africa, have a long way to go to hit that mark. In Uganda, class size often exceeds 100. In Chad it ranges from 70 to 200 children. The World Bank has determined that a 40-to-1 ratio should be the goal of countries as part of the Education for All (EFA) Fast Track Initiative.

In addition, many schools are understaffed, especially in rural areas. Moreover, teachers do not always show up at school. Allowed absences may amount to 20 percent of the school year. Worse, some teachers simply move to cities while still collecting their salaries, and civil service rules often make it difficult to fire nonperformers. In some countries, up to 10 percent of schools may be empty, their teachers elsewhere. Such waste absorbs resources that the majority of dedicated teachers could have put to use.

> Boyle, Siobhan, et al. 2002. "Reaching the Poor: The 'Costs' of Sending Children to School." London: DfID Education Papers series.
>
> UNICEF. 2001. *Fourth Consolidated Report to the Government of Norway on the UNICEF African Girls' Education Initiative.* New York: UNICEF Program Division/Education Section.
>
> Deininger, Klaus. 2003. "Does Cost of Schooling Affect Enrollment by the Poor? Universal Primary Education in Uganda." *Economics of Education Review* 22 (3): 291–305.

- **Indonesia's experience shows more teachers, not just more schools, are key to expanding boys' and girls' enrollment.** When Indonesia built thousands of new schools in a drive to increase enrollment, it also provided additional qualified and trained teachers to maintain class-size norms. As a result, despite rapid expansion in the school system, student academic performance held up.

> Duflo, Esther. 2001. "Schooling and Labor Market Consequences of School Construction in Indonesia: Evidence from an Unusual Policy Experiment." *American Economic Review* 91 (4): 795–813.

2. Improve Teachers' Education and Training

Many studies link teachers' own education and training levels with enrollment and attainment, especially among girls. But in many developing countries, teachers themselves lack sufficient education. Moreover, teacher training programs are often scarce or weak.

- **Research from Africa and Asia shows the importance of hiring teachers who have sufficient education in the fields they teach.** Teachers' own education consistently affects children's learning. Teacher training does not always compensate; it often focuses on teaching methods. Making sure teachers meet minimum education qualifications may be particularly important in low-income countries, where teachers may not even have a complete secondary education and so may have subject knowledge that does not far exceed their students'. A study in Pakistan found that only three of five teachers could pass primary school math exams, compared with two out of five of their students.

Ridker, Ronald G., ed. 1997. "Determinants of Educational Achievement and Attainment in Africa: Findings from Nine Case Studies." SD Publication Series, Technical Paper No. 62. Washington, D.C.: USAID.

Warwick, Donald, and Fernando Reimers. 1995. *Hope or Despair? Learning in Pakistan's Primary Schools.* Westport: Praeger.

- **A Swaziland study found that teacher training helped raise girls' enrollments to boys' level.** The government hired more teachers and trained the teacher corps in curriculum content as well as participatory learning, giving them objectives for each lesson. The government set up regional resource centers, trained professors for its three teachers' colleges, and improved feedback systems for teachers. By 1990, most teachers were qualified. Enrollments climbed, with girls participating as much as boys. By 1997, three-fourths of Swazi children had completed grade 4, and almost half went on to secondary school.

Gilmore, Julianne. 1997. "Phoenix Rising." USAID Technical Paper No. 76. Washington, D.C.: USAID.

- **Angola's Back to School program trains more teachers to promote post-conflict enrollment.** The prolonged civil conflict in Angola kept many teachers away from school. Angola expanded teacher training in former conflict zones and saw primary school enrollments surge. About 5,000 teachers, many of them women, received short, emergency training. For 2004, the government aims to train enough teachers to achieve a 90 percent increase in enrollment in the first four grades.

UNICEF. 2003. *State of the World's Children 2004.* New York: UNICEF.

- **Studies find good training enables young, undereducated women to teach primary school effectively, if temporarily.** In countries such as Bangladesh, Pakistan, and India, girls often have to be taught by women, and with few women literate, some provinces have relaxed age and education requirements to hire enough teachers. This happens particularly in remote rural areas, where many women are reluctant to be posted, so that young women from local communities are needed. Yet these young women have proved that they can teach effectively at the primary level if they have enough training and community support. It helps to provide programmed curricula and lesson plans, and coming from the communities they serve helps these teachers reach the children. Many such efforts involve NGOs as well as government.

Kim, Jooseop, Harold Alderman, and Peter Orazem. 1998. "Can Cultural Barriers Be Overcome in Girls' Schooling? The Community Support Program in Rural Balochistan." Working Paper Series on Impact Evaluation of Education Reforms Paper No. 10, World Bank Development Research Group. Washington, D.C.: World Bank.

Khandkher, Shahidur. 1996. "Education Achievements and School Efficiency in Rural Bangladesh." World Bank Discussion Paper No. 319. Washington, D.C.: World Bank.

Rugh, Andrea. 2000. "Starting Now: Strategies for Helping Girls Complete Primary." SAGE Project. Washington, D.C.: Academy for Educational Development.

World Bank. 1997. "Pakistan: New Approaches to Education: The Northern Areas Community School Program." Washington, D.C.: World Bank.

- **Brazil's major national effort to train teachers reduced the ranks of the untrained to less than 5 percent.** The effort was undertaken in conjunction with broad-based education reforms, including a revamped curriculum.

  Delannoy, Francoise, and Guilherme Sedlacek. 2000. "Brazil: Teachers' Development and Incentives: A Strategic Framework." World Bank Report 20408-BR. Washington, D.C.: World Bank.

3. Provide a Curriculum That Equips Children for the Twenty-first Century, with More Focus on Math, Science, and Problem Solving

Curricula in many countries are outmoded and highly limited, particularly in math and science. Some help perpetuate gender stereotyping or even ethnic conflict. Many countries are revamping curricula and struggling to improve mathematics, reading and writing in local languages, and critical foreign languages. Beyond these basics, more attention to science and life skills, such as how to avoid HIV/AIDS, is clearly helpful. Logic suggests that parents may be more willing to send children to school if they feel it will help their children cope in the future and raise their living standards. This is especially important for convincing parents to send their girls to school when demand for female education is more fragile.

- **More relevant and skill-based curricula are associated with higher enrollments, several country studies show.** For instance, in Brazil, Swaziland, and Uganda, as part of broader education reforms, curricula were revamped to focus more on issues of greater relevance, to broaden beyond basics, and to encourage problem solving. Enrollments of boys and girls increased with these reforms, but it is not possible to separate the impact of curriculum reform.

  Gilmore, Julianne. 1997. "Phoenix Rising." USAID Technical Paper No. 76. Washington, D.C.: USAID.

  Delannoy, Francoise, and Guilherme Sedlacek. 2000. "Brazil: Teachers' Development and Incentives: A Strategic Framework." World Bank Report 20408-BR. Washington, D.C.: World Bank.

- **In Kenya, parents are more willing to pay to send girls to school if girls can study science.** A study shows proportionally fewer girls than boys gained admission to government schools, and parents spend more to send girls to private secondary schools. Three times as many girls in private schools study science as do girls in the less costly government schools, suggesting that parents prefer for their girls to be studying math and science.

BOX **10**

The Importance of Randomized Evaluations in Determining the Success of Educational Interventions

Led by Harvard economist Michael Kremer and MIT economists Abhijit Banerjee and Esther Duflo, an increasing number of studies in recent years have specifically incorporated a randomized approach to the project and evaluation design. Randomized evaluations carefully choose in advance a suitable control group (that is, a group that, in the absence of the program, would have had outcomes similar to those who were exposed to the program). This allows for the determination of a statistically significant difference between the two groups in the outcomes the program intends to affect in a given economic and social context.

In practice, the results of randomized evaluations can often be quite different from the results estimated by other evaluation practices. For example, evaluations conducted without randomized methods typically suggest that providing schools with textbooks improves learning. Results from a recent randomized evaluation in Kenya, however, point to a more subtle picture. Providing additional textbooks increased test scores, but only among students who were at the top of their class prior to the program; the textbook provision did not affect the scores of the bottom 60 percent of students. It seems that many students may have failed to benefit from the textbooks because Kenyan textbooks are in English (the official language of instruction), but English is most pupils' third language (after their mother tongue and Swahili).

Credible program evaluations are also important in determining a program's cost effectiveness.

Because of the limited resources available for educational systems in developing countries, a central and fundamental policy concern is the relative cost effectiveness of various interventions, and evaluations of cost effectiveness require credible estimates of a program's impact. A recent set of studies in Kenya was conducted using randomized evaluations and has allowed estimates of cost effectiveness for several types of educational programs. For example, deworming was found to be extraordinarily cost effective at only $3.50 per additional year of schooling.

The benefits of knowing which programs work most cost effectively extend far beyond any specific program, as the results of such evaluations offer guidance to donors, governments, and international organizations in their ongoing search for effective programs. Given that randomized evaluations require a great deal of work and that relatively few randomized evaluations are currently being conducted, it is important that we encourage and finance randomized evaluations in the future in order to be confident that our policy decisions are reflecting what has been shown to work in improving female education.

Hanushek, Eric. 1995. "Interpreting Recent Research on Schooling in Developing Countries." *World Bank Research Observer* 10 (2): 227–46.

Glewwe, Paul, Michael Kremer, and Sylvie Moulin. 2002. "Textbooks and Test Scores: Evidence from a Prospective Evaluation in Kenya." Cambridge: Harvard University.

Miguel, Edward, and Michael Kremer. 2004. "Worms: Identifying Impacts on Education and Health in the Presence of Treatment Externalities." *Econometrica* 72 (1): 159–217.

Herz, Barbara, et al. 1991. "Letting Girls Learn: Promising Approaches in Primary and Secondary Education." World Bank Discussion Paper No. 133. Washington, D.C.: World Bank.

4. Provide Adequate Books and Supplies

In many low-income countries, even having one schoolbook per child is a luxury. In Rwanda, for example, four children share textbooks for math and language, and in Cape Verde, one-fifth of students have no textbooks. In some countries, learning materials are commonly locked up and seldom used (to prevent them from being used up). Where schools have few or hardly any books or learning materials, parents may not bother to send their children. Research is limited but suggests these inputs matter, particularly in parents' decisions to educate girls.

UNICEF. 2001. *Fourth Consolidated Report to the Government of Norway on the UNICEF African Girls' Education Initiative.* New York: UNICEF Program Division/Education Section.

Rugh, Andrea. 2000. "Starting Now: Strategies for Helping Girls Complete Primary." SAGE Project. Washington, D.C.: Academy for Educational Development.

- **A Peru study has found that providing textbooks raises girls' enrollments.** This study found that when free textbooks were supplied to primary schools, controlling for other influences, girls were 30 percent more likely to enroll, but no effect was recorded for boys' enrollments.

King, Elizabeth, and Rosemary Bellew. 1991. "Gains in the Education of Peruvian Women, 1940–1980." In Barbara Herz and Shahidur Khandkher, eds., "Women's Work, Education, and Family Welfare in Peru." World Bank Discussion Paper No. 116. Washington, D.C.: World Bank.

- **A multicountry study found that textbooks boost enrollment and achievement.** Provision of textbooks encourages girls' enrollments in Africa and South Asia and is one of the few interventions that promotes achievement (along with alternative learning programs and single-sex schools).

Rugh, Andrea. 2000. "Starting Now: Strategies for Helping Girls Complete Primary." SAGE Project. Washington, D.C.: Academy for Educational Development.

E. Setting Priorities

The experiences of three diverse countries that are making strong efforts to improve basic education provide good examples of how developing countries can set different priorities but still achieve significant progress toward universal education (see Appendix).

- **Uganda redirected resources to its education budget, cut school fees, and revamped the teacher corps.** President Yoweri Museveni made basic education a major focus, and, among other things, his government cut the defense budget in order to increase education expenditures, revamped a teacher corps plagued by chronic absences, raised teacher salaries sharply, modernized the curriculum (introducing education on HIV/AIDS), provided more textbooks, and cut school fees. Enrollment skyrocketed, but class size ballooned. The country is now addressing the problems associated with overcrowding and is working to address the associated quality issues.

  Bruns, Barbara, Alain Mingat, and Ramahatra Rakotomalala. 2003. "Achieving Universal Primary Education by 2015: A Chance for Every Child." Washington, D.C.: World Bank.

- **Indonesia achieved near universal enrollment by cutting school fees, building schools, and maintaining class size.** Education has been a presidential focus in Indonesia since the 1970s. The government cut school fees. Mobilizing oil revenues, it began a massive program to build schools in areas that lacked them, making sure the new schools also had qualified and trained teachers and enough books and learning materials—class size remained at 40 pupils. As the school system expanded, enrollments rose to approach 100 percent and children's learning scores were maintained. Further efforts are under way to improve education quality and learning.

  Duflo, Esther. 2001. "Schooling and Labor Market Consequences of School Construction in Indonesia: Evidence from an Unusual Policy Experiment." *American Economic Review* 91 (4): 795–813.

- **Brazil improved education spending and focused on equity, thanks to high-level political commitment.** The government undertook education reform in two phases during the 1990s. In the first phase, it focused on expanding access and ensuring that disadvantaged children had as much access, passing a constitutional amendment to equalize per-pupil spending and cross-subsidizing poorer areas. In the second phase, it concentrated on reforming the system and strengthening the teacher corps, increasing teacher qualifications, raising teacher salaries, and improving teacher training. Enrollments increased rapidly for both boys and girls, and learning indicators held stable. Further measures are under way in Brazil as well to improve education quality and learning.

  Delannoy, Francoise, and Guilherme Sedlacek. 2000. "Brazil: Teachers' Development and Incentives: A Strategic Framework." World Bank Report 20408-BR. Washington, D.C.: World Bank.

V. Getting the Job Done

The central policy question has moved beyond what works to educate girls and should now focus on how to build support for and provide affordable, quality education. Extensive research from countries that have undertaken reforms suggests that countries can make rapid progress and reach universal education, if they successfully address three critical components.

A. Leadership and Political Will at the Country Level

Although it is difficult to sort out the exact effect of leadership, experience in countries such as China, Morocco, Oman, Sri Lanka, and Uganda (and, on the negative side, countries such as Afghanistan) suggests government leadership in poor countries is key to raising the profile of girls' education and making progress on getting more girls in school. In these countries, among others, heads of government have spoken out strongly on the need to educate all children and made educating girls a high and a visible priority.

- **In Uganda, President Museveni in 1997 led a vigorous campaign to promote education for girls as well as boys** as part of the newly elected Ugandan government's policy of universal primary education. Uganda made education a budget priority, and education as a share of recurrent government expenditure increased from 11 percent to 22 percent between 1997 and 2002. If Uganda's education spending and increasing enrollment continue, the World Bank projects the country will achieve universal primary education by 2015.

    Bruns, Barbara, Alain Mingat, and Ramahatra Rakotomalala. 2003. "Achieving Universal Primary Education by 2015: A Chance for Every Child." Washington, D.C.: World Bank.

- **Enlisting leaders from other parts of society can also promote girls' enrollments,** particularly when it reinforces government leadership and community participation. Approaches include calls from religious leaders for girls' education; provision of education through religious authorities; television, radio, or theater programs; provision of supplies such as computers by business leaders or schools provided by employers; and political pressure from women's organizations (see Box 11).

Tietjen, Karen. 2000. "Multisector Support of Basic and Girls' Education." SAGE Project. Washington, D.C.: Academy for Educational Development.

Puryear, Jeffrey. M., ed. 1997. "Partners for Progress, Education and the Private Sector in Latin America and the Caribbean." Washington, D.C.: Inter-American Dialogue.

BOX **11**

Enlisting Civil Society to Improve Girls' Education

The business community has primarily focused on improving existing schools, for instance by supplying computers or other equipment. In some cases, however, major employers also provide schools for their employees' children. The business community also stands out in advocating for better education and in mobilizing its members in the effort. Business communities are supporting girls' education in a range of countries: Guatemala, India, Mexico, Morocco, Peru, Thailand, and Venezuela. Not only domestic firms but increasingly major international firms are joining this effort.

The religious community's focus has been on reaching poor children and often emphasizes religious instruction as well as basic academic subjects. In Islamic countries, Koranic schools are almost always found and may account for as much as one-fourth of students enrolled. The Roman Catholic Church also operates an extensive education system. A number of other religions also sponsor schools. Religious leaders have proved crucial in advocating for girls' education, especially where few girls have gone to school before; religious opposition to girls' education has, of course,

also proved formidable. In many places, however, religious leaders are willing to encourage girls' education if it can be provided in culturally acceptable ways.

The media are widely active in influencing girls' education. Distance learning through radio is increasingly being tried; it has shown promise in Latin America particularly. In every region, television, radio, and theater have helped to encourage girls' education through programs showing girls and women as role models in nontraditional jobs or by advocating for girls' education. Similarly the press has been active in every region. Of course, the media do not always support greater female education, but where they do, they are considered to have helped.

Women's organizations have pressed energetically for girls' education and focus particularly on disadvantaged girls, including girls from poor families, girls in remote areas, and girls who work in exploitative or appalling situations. Women's organizations have perhaps been strongest in Africa but are active in every region.

B. Developing Comprehensive, Nationally Owned Strategies

In April 2000, more than 180 countries pledged at the UN World Education Forum in Dakar, Senegal, to the Dakar Framework of Action: to achieve universal education by 2015 with a specific commitment to ensuring girls full and equal access to quality education. At the core of these commitments was the notion of a global compact. Poor countries committed to develop comprehensive, nationally owned strategies for achieving universal education that tackle fundamental reforms to improve access, quality, and efficiency in the public education system, to allocate increased domestic resources to these national plans, and to set performance targets by which to gauge progress over time. In return, donors committed that where such credible, accountable plans and domestic resource commitments exist, no country would fail due to lack of resources.

Research and experience confirm that such a global compact is the right approach. It is grounded in the basic idea that donor assistance is most effective when it empowers those who are committed to taking responsibility for addressing their own challenges. While it is critical, of course, to identify and tackle squarely the education reforms that are needed to give children access and improve education quality—reforms that are profoundly difficult to implement—countries as diverse as Bangladesh, Brazil, China, Indonesia, and Uganda have successfully designed and begun to implement such credible, comprehensive national education plans. Research suggests that such national strategies can catalyze rapid and substantial improvements in girls' (and boys') education because they provide a consensus on which to build, a guide to policy and implementation, and a gauge for progress.

> Sperling, Gene. 2001. "Toward Universal Education: Making a Promise and Keeping It." *Foreign Affairs* 80 (5): 7–13.

> Herz, Barbara. 2002. "Universal Basic Education: What Works." Paper prepared for the Coalition for Basic Education. Washington, D.C.: Academy for Educational Development.

- **To support this global compact, the Education for All Fast Track Initiative has developed a new financing structure and process for poor countries to demonstrate their commitment to a country-owned, accountable national education strategy.** The initiative, coordinated by the World Bank, started with a first round of 18 countries in 2002. They were declared eligible for "fast track" funding, contingent on submitting a national plan. In November 2002, 7 countries—Burkina Faso, Guinea, Guyana, Honduras, Mauritania, Nicaragua, and Niger—had their plans officially approved, and in March 2003 another 3 countries received approval: Gambia, Mozambique, and Yemen. Most recently, Ghana and Vietnam were approved. As of November 2003, the process was opened to more developing countries.

Bruns, Barbara, Alain Mingat, and Ramahatra Rakotomalala. 2003. "Achieving Universal Primary Education by 2015: A Chance for Every Child." Washington, D.C.: World Bank.

- **The World Bank has developed guidelines for national education plans based on the class sizes and fiscal targets associated with successful reforms in poor countries.** Key elements of national plans include ensuring that government spending on education is at least 20 percent of the national recurrent budget; ensuring that 50 percent of education spending goes to primary education; keeping repetition rates lower than 10 percent; reducing class sizes to fewer than 40 pupils per teacher; and abolishing fees for primary school.

  Bruns, Barbara, Alain Mingat, and Ramahatra Rakotomalala. 2003. "Achieving Universal Primary Education by 2015: A Chance for Every Child." Washington, D.C.: World Bank.

- **Beyond these guidelines, the most successful national plans have incorporated strong, credible budget transparency and antifraud provisions.** To achieve the necessary but difficult education reforms described above in Section IV, research suggests that several kinds of measures are usually necessary, as the experiences of Brazil, Indonesia, and Uganda have shown (see Appendix).

  - **Public-sector reform.** National plans should streamline management of public schools to increase transparency and accountability. Uganda, Indonesia, and Pakistan, among others, have undertaken major managerial and civil service reforms as part of their national education strategies to combat poor governance and achieve basic standards in teachers' performance and school operation.

  - **Encourage decentralization.** In supporting the national public education system, national plans should look for opportunities to encourage decentralization to local schools and communities to reduce midlevel bureaucracy and encourage efficiency. Many countries ranging from Indonesia to India, Pakistan, Brazil, and Nicaragua are working to decentralize; returns are not yet in, but early signs are promising.

  - **Set specific performance targets** year by year by which to gauge progress. This inspires confidence among donors and key stakeholders within the country.

  - **Include comprehensive monitoring and evaluation** components, including, where appropriate, increased use of controlled policy experimentation as described above. Although country circumstances vary, successful reforms of public education tend to involve a package of such measures.

    Moseley, Stephen. 2003. "Testimony to the Foreign Operations Subcommittee of the US House of Representatives Committee on Appropriations." May 14.

    Sperling, Gene, and Tom Hart. 2003. "A Better Way to Fight Poverty." *Foreign Affairs* 82 (2): 9–14.

- **Participation of local communities, along with NGOs and private actors, can greatly strengthen these national strategies, driving a new paradigm for effective partnership.** These partnerships take effort to establish but are encouraged in the Education for All framework and are currently working to boost enrollments, particularly for girls. The most promising design includes the following:

  - Government providing overall guidance, curriculum, books, uniforms, and teacher salaries—and backing up locally managed schools with a lean but supportive system.

  - Communities and parents offering significant input and support, often facilitated by a local NGO that helps mobilize support for a decision to educate girls as well as boys, and design and run local school-system functions. Typically in these arrangements, parents select or help select the teachers, enforce teachers' attendance, help maintain the school buildings, and in some cases even provide a place for a school, all in close partnership with government.

  - In many countries, the private-school systems, including religious schools and some community schools, can be an important partner. They are increasingly reaching marginalized populations and providing more comprehensive services in some cases. But the private system cannot be relied on to fill the gaps in schooling the hard-to-reach.

    Herz, Barbara. 2002. "Universal Basic Education: What Works." Paper prepared for the Coalition for Basic Education. Washington, D.C.: Academy for Educational Development.

C. Mobilizing Internal and External Resources

Experience has clearly shown that the extent of the reform necessary to increase girls' enrollment and educational attainment and achieve quality universal education is beyond the capacity of most poor-country governments. Developing countries need to make firm commitments to a national strategy, including the commitment of significant resources, but also need a clear mechanism for securing external resources so that positive reforms are sustained and they do not face backsliding. For example, when the Tanzanian government took the bold step to end school fees in 2000, it saw enrollments double, yet was unprepared, even with some donor support, to keep class size below effective levels.

1. Mobilizing Internal Resources

- **A 56-country analysis established a strong relationship between adequate public spending and boosting primary enrollments.** An analysis of education spending patterns in 56 developing countries found that those countries that had achieved universal primary school completion spent more on primary education—1.7 percent of gross domestic product (GDP) on average, versus a 1.4 percent average across all countries studied—and maintained reasonable unit costs for facilities, supplies, and teacher salaries (see Figure 3).

Fredriksen, Birger. 2002. "Is Universal Primary Completion Achievable in 2015?" Washington, D.C.: World Bank.

2. Mobilizing External Resources

While a domestic resource commitment is key, a clear commitment of external donor resources is an essential component of a viable global compact. The traditional debate over whether money is or is not the central problem for achieving universal education presents a false choice. Few disagree that current levels of funding are woefully inadequate to achieve the goal of universal education by 2015, considering the depth of the education crisis in so many poor countries, especially

FIGURE 3

Domestic Resources Are Not a Silver Bullet, but a Clear Association Exists Between Primary Completion Rates and Education Spending

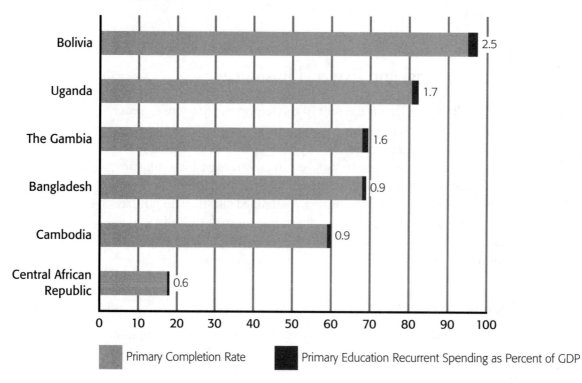

Source: Bruns et al. 2003.

80

in Africa. Currently, donor assistance for primary education in poor countries is estimated at $1.4 billion annually. What is truly needed is a credible ex ante commitment of donor resources contingent on countries' developing and demonstrating significant progress toward the types of national education strategies described above. Experience confirms that such a commitment can act as a powerful tool both to empower the willing—countries like Uganda that have already made significant strides toward universal education and countries like Tanzania that have taken important and politically difficult steps such as ending fees for primary school—and to empower forward-looking education ministers in more hesitant counties who are trying to capture the attention and support of their finance ministers and heads of state.

> Sperling, Gene. 2003. "Toward a Global Compact on Universal Education." Testimony before the Foreign Operations Subcommittee of the U.S. House of Representatives Committee on Appropriations. May 14.

- **The external resources required to achieve universal basic education are at least an additional $5 billion–$10 billion per year.** Estimates of the total financing gap for achieving universal primary education in developing countries range from $10 billion to $15 billion per year. The portion of that gap that poor countries will not be able to finance on their own was estimated by the World Bank at $3.7 billion per year through 2015, a conservative estimate. The UN Educational, Scientific, and Cultural Organization (UNESCO), accounting for additional costs, projected that $5.6 billion in external resources is needed annually to achieve universal primary education. If country strategies aim for universal basic education (which can include more grades than primary) and effective but expensive programs like stipends to get more girls in school or addressing HIV/AIDS, the external resource requirement may actually be closer to $10 billion than $5 billion.

> UNESCO. 2002. *EFA Global Monitoring Report: Is the World on Track?* Paris: UNESCO.

> World Bank. 2004. "Education for All Fast Track Initiative Progress Report." April 25. Washington, D.C.: World Bank.

- **Unfortunately, such a strong contingent commitment has not been made real for the poor countries in the EFA Fast Track Initiative.** The first 10 countries to meet the Fast Track criteria for funding have received commitments totaling less than $300 million per year. This is well below the countries' projected needs in their national education plans, and barely what the first 7 countries had requested. The original needs estimate for the first 7 countries alone was $430 million over 3 years, which was subsequently revised downward to $315 million. Despite articulating their continuing commitment to the process, the donors have yet to provide any credible assurance to countries in the EFA process that if they follow through on designing comprehensive national education strategies, donors funds will support them.

Sperling, Gene. 2003. "Donor Reactions to the Education for All Initiative." Paper prepared for the UN Millennium Project Task Force on Education and Gender Equality. July.

- **High-level political commitment from G8 countries could assure the necessary financial resources.** The next two meetings of the group of eight highly industrialized countries (G8)—the June 2004 meeting hosted by the United States and the 2005 meeting hosted by the United Kingdom—may provide a critically important window of opportunity for generating the kind of political and financial support necessary to turn the EFA's progress to date into a true global compact on universal education. Such a commitment from donor countries can be critical to the success of country plans and to the credibility of the EFA goal as much more than another lofty, but empty, promise.

VI. Conclusion:
A Problem
with a Known Cure

An overwhelming body of research demonstrates that investing in girls' education delivers high returns for economic growth and broad benefits ranging from sustainable families to disease prevention to women's well-being. Educating girls as well as boys is an achievable goal and attainable in the near term, if substantial resources are matched with comprehensive nationally owned plans for education reform that include measures of accountability and a commitment to ensure all children are in school. Realizing steady improvements also comes down to national and international commitment, political leadership, and an emphasis on tailoring policies to local circumstances to meet the distinct challenges each country faces.

In countries where girls' enrollment rates are especially low, economic constraints and social custom can often combine to leave parents feeling that the costs of educating girls are higher than those for boys and the benefits more distant and uncertain. It is particularly important to reduce the costs to parents of educating girls.

The costs of education to governments are also substantial. Poor countries face severe resource constraints, so that financing even top-priority basic education programs can prove difficult. To this end, where countries commit to effective and efficient plans for education reform, and those reforms show genuine impact for both girls and boys, donors should provide substantial assistance.

Serious efforts, even in countries with highly constrained resources, are likely to yield impressive results, both for educational outcomes and for the society as a whole. In short, there may be no better investment for the health and development of poor countries around the world than investments to educate girls.

Appendix:
Country Case Studies

Brazil's Reach for Universal Basic Education. In the past decade, Brazil transformed its education system, tackling inefficiency and uneven opportunity for poor children. It now has one of the more promising systems in the developing world—a noteworthy accomplishment given Brazil's population and vast terrain. In its first major set of reforms, Brazil focused on expanding access to education by increasing financing, rationalizing overlapping responsibilities among different levels of government, and addressing quality. A constitutional amendment, passed in 1995, established a yearly per-pupil spending floor to reduce differences between poorer and better-off areas. Brazil used national tax revenues to cross-subsidize poorer areas and improved the efficiency of expenditures.

It then launched a second set of reforms to improve quality. It established a national standardized student-assessment system and a new national curriculum (the federal government sets guidelines, but states, municipalities, and even local schools can adapt them). The curriculum includes a wider range of subjects and stresses problem solving, independent learning, and critical thinking. With the federal government, 27 states, and some 5,500 municipalities all involved in schools, Brazil had an overlapping system with confusing jurisdictions. Legislation enacted in 1996 sorted out responsibilities. The federal government now sets policy and guarantees equity and quality. The states lead in secondary education, the municipalities in preschool and primary education. Brazil has also strengthened its teacher corps—some 1.6 million people. It increased teacher salaries 13 percent in 1997–98 and provided generous pension benefits. It also set higher qualifications for teacher certification. Over 1997–99, the proportion of teachers with no more than a secondary education fell from 44 percent to 38 percent. The government set a national framework for teacher training, and the number of untrained teachers declined to less than 5 percent. Brazil also began civil service reform, allowing dismissal based on performance.

By 1997, Brazil's net enrollment rate reached 100 percent for boys and 94 percent for girls, compared with 82 percent and 79 percent in 1980. Of course, challenges remain. Children's test scores have not improved—though with such rapid expansion, just avoiding a decline is an accomplishment. Performance remains below national goals and varies with the type of school and poverty level. Finally, the need for more effective teaching persists, and the demand for teachers is growing.

> Delannoy, Francoise, and Guilherme Sedlacek. 2000. "Brazil: Teachers' Development and Incentives: A Strategic Framework." World Bank Report 20408-BR. Washington, D.C.: World Bank.

Indonesia's Drive for Basic Education. During 1973–78, the Indonesian government undertook Presidential Instruction, or INPRES, programs to improve equity across its far-flung islands. Starting with a gross enrollment rate in primary schools of about 60 percent, Indonesia gave priority to basic education and began one of the world's fastest programs of school construction. Between 1973–74 and 1978–79, 61,807 primary schools were built at a cost of over $500 million (in 1990 U.S. dollars), or 1.5 percent of Indonesia's 1973 gross national product (GNP). Mobilizing oil revenues to finance the programs, real expenditures on regional development more than doubled over 1973–80.

Critically, the program did not stop at building schools. The government worked to maintain quality as the school system grew. Each new school was designed for 120 students and 3 teachers. Once a school was built, the government recruited teachers and paid them, and ran a teacher training program in parallel with the school building effort. Across Indonesia, the proportion of teachers meeting minimum qualifications did not decline significantly over 1971–78, and the student-teacher ratio stayed at about 40:1. In 1978 the government also cut primary school fees.

Today Indonesia's net enrollment rates for both boys and girls approach 100 percent. Nine of ten men and four of five women are literate, and educational attainment averages more than eight years. Each school built per 1,000 children led to an average of 0.12–0.19 years more schooling for the first group of children fully exposed to the program, which later boosted their earnings. In Indonesia's open society, these measures worked to enroll both boys and girls. Concerns about education quality remain, however, and girls face problems related to gender stereotyping in Indonesia, as in most countries.

> Duflo, Esther. 2001. "Schooling and Labor Market Consequences of School Construction in Indonesia: Evidence from an Unusual Policy Experiment." *American Economic Review* 91 (4): 795–813.

Uganda's Education Reforms: Balancing Access and Quality. In 1997 the Ugandan government announced a new policy of universal primary education (UPE), and President Yoweri Museveni led a campaign to promote education for girls as well as boys. To reach UPE, the government introduced fundamental reforms that included providing free schooling for up to four children per household and other measures to improve quality. It removed "ghost" teachers from teacher rolls and required that teachers pass proficiency tests, which reduced rolls further. Teachers who remained and their principals were given improved training, covering new and established subjects. Teacher salaries were increased dramatically, from about $8 to $72 per month. Curriculum was changed: important efforts were introduced to teach about HIV/AIDS, for example. The government also ended an old textbook monopoly, liberalized procurement, and earmarked 3 percent of the recurrent budget for books and materials. Some 1.5 million new books are now in students' hands.

To finance the UPE effort, the government increased education budgets sharply, raising education's share of the national budget from 22 percent to 31 percent in 1999 and cutting the defense budget in the process. The education budget thus grew from 1.6 percent of GNP to over 4 percent. The government also increased the portion of the education budget going to basic education to 70 percent, trimming university subsidies. Donors helped, covering about 30 percent of the UPE budget. Debt relief provided other resources.

In the late 1990s, research shows primary school enrollments doubled, reaching 6.5 million by 2000. The net enrollment rate rose from 54 percent to over 90 percent (comparable to East Asian countries with higher incomes)—a stunning accomplishment for a low-income country emerging from civil war. Still, the picture is not rosy. Class size has ballooned: the student-teacher ratio exceeds 100:1. Another 40,000 teachers and 26,000 classrooms are needed. Concerns for quality are rising. Moreover, although girls' as well as boys' enrollments have risen, in some areas disparities between girls and boys and between rural and urban children are worse, suggesting that more deliberate efforts to diagnose and address girls' specific needs would be helpful.

Bruns, Barbara, Alain Mingat, and Ramahatra Rakotomalala. 2003. "Achieving Universal Primary Education by 2015: A Chance for Every Child." Washington, D.C.: World Bank.

Gilmore, Julianne. 1997. "Phoenix Rising." USAID Technical Paper No. 76. Washington, D.C.: USAID.

References

Afridi, Zahid. 2000. *Pakistan's Primary Education Quality Improvement Program.* Washington, D.C.: Academy for Educational Development.

Alderman, Harold, and Elizabeth M. King. 1998. "Gender Differences in Parental Investment in Education." *Structural Change and Economic Dynamics* 9 (4): 453–68.

Alderman, Harold, Peter Orazem, and Elizabeth Paterno. 1996. "School Quality, School Cost, and the Public/Private Choices of Low-Income Households in Pakistan." Impact Evaluation of Education Reform Working Paper No. 2, World Bank Development Research Group. Washington, D.C.: World Bank.

Angrist, Joshua, et al. 2002. "Vouchers for Private Schooling in Colombia: Evidence from a Randomized Natural Experiment." *American Economic Review* 92 (5): 1535–58.

Assad, R., and F. El-Hamidi. 2001. "Is All Work the Same? A Comparison of the Determinants of Female Participation and Hours of Work in Various Employment States in Egypt." In E. M. Cinar, ed., *The Economics of Women and Work in the Middle East and North Africa.* Amsterdam: Elsevier.

Bakhteari, Quratul Ain. 1997. "Report Submitted to AID on Completion of Contract for Technical Assistance, Beneficiary Participation to Balochistan Primary Education Department Programme, 1994–97." Washington, D.C.: Academy for Educational Development.

Banerjee, Abhijit, et al. 2003. "Remedying Education: Evidence from Two Randomized Experiments in India." Cambridge: Massachusetts Institute of Technology.

Banerjee, Abhijit, Suraj Jacob, and Michael Kremer, with Jenny Lanjouw and Peter Lanjouw. 2000. "Promoting School Participation in Rural Rajasthan: Results from Some Prospective Trials." Cambridge: Harvard University.

Banerjee, Abhijit, and Michael Kremer. 2002. "Teacher-Student Ratios and School Performance in Udaipur, India: A Prospective Evaluation." Cambridge: Harvard University.

Barro, Robert J. 1999. "Determinants of Democracy." *Journal of Political Economy* 107 (6): S158–83.

———. 1991. "Economic Growth in a Cross Section of Countries." *Quarterly Journal of Economics* 106 (2): 407–43.

Barro, Robert, and Jong Wha Lee. 1996. "International Measures of Schooling Years and Schooling Quality." *American Economic Review* 86 (2): 218–23.

Basu, Alaka. 1992. *Culture, the Status of Women, and Demographic Behavior: Illustrated with the Case of India.* Oxford: Clarendon.

Basu, Ananya, and Elizabeth M. King. 2001. "Does Education Promote Growth and Democracy? Some Evidence from East Asia and Latin America." Washington, D.C.: World Bank.

Becker, Gary. 1981. *A Treatise on the Family.* Cambridge: Harvard University Press.

Behrman, Jere R. 1991. "Investing in Female Education for Development." U.S. Agency for International Development (USAID) Genesys Special Studies No. 5. Washington, D.C.: USAID.

Behrman, Jere, et al. 1999. "Women's Schooling, Home Teaching, and Economic Growth." *Journal of Political Economy* 107 (4): 682–719.

Behrman, Jere, and Anil Deolalikar. 1995. "Are There Differential Returns to Schooling by Gender? The Case of Indonesian Labor Markets." *Oxford Bulletin of Economics and Statistics* 57 (1): 97–117.

Benveniste, L., and P. J. McEwan. 2000. "Constraints to Implementing Educational Innovations: The Case of Multi-Grade Schools." *International Review of Education* 46 (1–2): 31–48.

Berrera, Albino. 1990. "The Role of Maternal Schooling and Its Interaction with Public Health Programs in Child Health Production." *Journal of Development Economics* 32 (1): 69–91.

Bils, Mark, and Peter Klenow. 2000. "Does Schooling Cause Growth?" *American Economic Review* 90 (5): 1160–83.

Biraimah, Karen Coffyn. 1980. "Different Knowledge for Different Folks: Knowledge Distribution in a Togolese Secondary School." In Philip G. Altbock, Robert F. Arnove, and Gail P. Kelly, eds., *Comparative Education.* New York: Macmillan.

Birdsall, Nancy, and Jere Behrman. 1991. "Why Do Males Earn More Than Females in Urban Brazil: Earnings Discrimination or Job Discrimination?" In Nancy Birdsall and Richard Sabot, eds., *Unfair Advantage: Labor Market Discrimination in Developing Countries.* Washington, D.C.: World Bank.

Bloom, David E., and David Canning. 1999. "The Demographic Transition and Economic Growth in the Middle East and North Africa." Paper presented at the Fourth Annual Conference of the Middle East Institute and the World Bank on Population Challenges and Economic Growth: Middle East and North Africa. Washington, D.C. April 14.

Bobonis, Gustavo, Edward Miguel, and Charu Sharma. 2002. "Iron Supplementation and Early Childhood Development: A Randomized Evaluation in India." Berkeley: University of California.

Boyle, Siobhan, et al. 2002. "Reaching the Poor: The 'Costs' of Sending Children to School." London: DfID Education Papers series.

Bruns, Barbara, Alain Mingat, and Ramahatra Rakotomalala. 2003. "Achieving Universal Primary Education by 2015: A Chance for Every Child." Washington, D.C.: World Bank.

Buvinic, Mayra. 1995. "Investing in Women." International Center for Research on Women (ICRW) Policy Series No. 2. Washington, D.C.: ICRW.

Cameron, L. A., J. Malcolm Dowling, and Christopher Worswick. 2001. "Education and Labor Market Participation of Women in Asia: Evidence from Five Countries." *Economic Development and Cultural Change* 49 (3): 461–77.

Cardiff, P. W. 1997. "The 1995–6 Household Income, Expenditure, and Consumption Survey. Final Analysis Report." In Ronald Ridker, ed., *Determinants of Educational Achievement and Attainment in Africa: Findings from Nine Case Studies.* Washington, D.C.: USAID.

Chabbott, Collette. 1998. *Egypt Primary School Assessment: Annotated Bibliography.* Washington, D.C.: USAID.

Chang, Mae Chu, and Guilherme Sedlacek. 1996. "Improving Basic Education in Pakistan." World Bank Report 14960-PAK. Washington, D.C.: World Bank.

Churcher, Christine. 2002. "Models for Promoting EFA: What's Working, What's Not?" Presentation to Conference at Center for Universal Education. Washington, D.C. June 11.

Coalition for Health and Education Rights. 2002. "User Fees: The Right to Education and Health Denied." Policy Brief. New York: Coalition for Health and Education Rights.

Crossette, Barbara. 2002. "Population Estimates Fall as Poor Women Assert Control." *New York Times.* March 10, A3.

Das Gupta, Monica. 1987. "Selective Discrimination against Female Children in Rural Punjab, India." *Population and Development Review* 13 (1): 77–100.

Deininger, Klaus. 2003. "Does Cost of Schooling Affect Enrollment by the Poor? Universal Primary Education in Uganda." *Economics of Education Review* 22 (3): 291–305.

Delamonica, Enrique, Santosh Mehrotra, and Jan Vandemoortele. 2001. "Education for All Is Affordable: A Minimum Global Cost Estimate." New York: UNICEF.

Delannoy, Francoise, and Guilherme Sedlacek. 2000. "Brazil: Teachers' Development and Incentives: A Strategic Framework." World Bank Report 20408-BR. Washington, D.C.: World Bank.

Deolalikar, Anil B. 1993. "Gender Differences in the Returns to Schooling and in School Enrollment Rates in Indonesia." *Journal of Human Resources* 28 (4): 899–932.

De Walque, Damien. 2004. "How Does Educational Attainment Affect the Risk of Being Infected by HIV/AIDS? Evidence from a General Population Cohort in Rural Uganda." World Bank Development Research Group Working Paper. Washington, D.C.: World Bank. March.

Dollar, David, and Roberta Gatti. 1999. "Gender Inequality, Income, and Growth: Are Good Times Good for Women?" World Bank Policy Research Report on Gender and Development, Working Paper Series No. 1. Washington, D.C.: World Bank.

Duflo, Esther. 2003. "Scaling Up and Evaluation." Proceedings of the Annual Bank Conference on Development Economics, Bangalore. Washington, D.C.: World Bank. May 21–23.

———. 2001. "Schooling and Labor Market Consequences of School Construction in Indonesia: Evidence from an Unusual Policy Experiment." *American Economic Review* 91 (4): 795–813.

Duflo, Esther, and Michael Kremer. 2003. "Use of Randomization in the Evaluation of Development Effectiveness." Paper prepared for the Fifth Biennial World Bank Conference on Evaluation and Development. "Evaluating Development Effectiveness: Challenges and the Way Forward." Washington, D.C. July 15–16.

Dugger, Celia. 2004. "Brazil Pays Parents to Help Poor Be Pupils, Not Wage Earners." *New York Times.* January 3, A1.

Duraisamy, P. 2002. "Changes in Returns to Education in India, 1983–94: By Gender, Age-Cohort, and Location." *Economics of Education Review* 21 (6): 609–22.

Esim, S. 2001. "Why Women Earn Less: Gender-Based Factors Affecting the Earnings of Self-Employed Women in Turkey." In E. M. Cinar, ed., *The Economics of Women and Work in the Middle East and North Africa.* Amsterdam: Elsevier.

Ethiopian Ministry of Education. 2002. "Education Sector Development Program: 2002/03–2004/05." Addis Ababa. May.

————. 1980. "Gender Analysis of Primary School Textbooks."

Filmer, Deon. 2000. "The Structure of Social Disparities in Education: Gender and Wealth." Policy Research Working Paper No. 2268, World Bank Development Research Group/Poverty Reduction and Economic Management Network. Washington, D.C.: World Bank.

————. 1999. "The Structure of Social Disparities in Education: Gender and Wealth." Policy Research Report on Gender and Development, Working Paper Series No. 5, World Bank Development Research Group/Poverty and Human Resources. Washington, D.C.: World Bank. May.

Filmer, Deon, and Lant Pritchett. 1999. "The Effect of Household Wealth on Educational Attainment." *Population and Development Review* 25 (1): 85–120.

Fiske, Edward. 1996. *Decentralization of Education: Politics and Consensus.* Washington, D.C.: World Bank.

Forum for African Women Educationalists (FAWE). 2001. "Girls' Education and Poverty Eradication: FAWE's Response." Presentation to the Third United Nations Conference on the Least Developed Countries. Brussels, Belgium. May 10–20.

————. 1997. "Is Your Daughter Safe in School?" *FAWE News* 5 (3): 6–8.

Foster, Andrew, and Mark Rosenzweig. 1996. "Technical Change and Human-Capital Returns and Investments: Evidence from the Green Revolution." *American Economic Review* 86 (4): 931–53.

Fredriksen, Birger. 2002a. "Education for All Children by 2015: What Will It Take to Keep the Promise?" Paper presented at the World Bank Annual Conference on Development Economics. Oslo. June 24–26.

————. 2002b. "Is Universal Primary Completion Achievable in 2015?" Washington, D.C.: World Bank.

Fuller, Bruce. 1986. "Raising School Quality in Developing Countries: What Investments Boost Learning?" World Bank Discussion Paper No. 2. Washington, D.C.: World Bank.

Gachukia, E., W. M. Kabira, and M. Masinjila. 1992. "Meeting the Basic Learning Needs of Adolescent Mothers in Kenya: A Situation Analysis." Nairobi: International Childhood Development Centre and UNICEF Kenya Country Office.

Gage, Anastasia, Elisabeth Sommerfelt, and Andrea Piani. 1997. "Household Structure and Childhood Immunization in Niger and Nigeria." *Demography* 34 (2): 195–309.

Gallant, M., and E. Maticka-Tyndale. 2003. "School-Based HIV Prevention Programmes for African Youth." *Social Science and Medicine* 58 (7): 337–51.

Gertler, Paul, and Paul Glewwe. 1992. "The Willingness to Pay for Education for Daughters in Contrast to Sons: Evidence from Rural Peru." *World Bank Economic Review* 6 (1): 171–88.

Gilmore, Julianne. 1997. "Phoenix Rising." USAID Technical Paper No. 76. Washington, D.C.: USAID.

Glewwe, Paul, et al. Forthcoming. "Retrospective vs. Prospective Analyses of School Inputs: The Case of Flip Charts in Kenya." *Journal of Development Economics.*

Glewwe, Paul, Michael Kremer, and Sylvie Moulin. 2002. "Textbooks and Test Scores: Evidence from a Prospective Evaluation in Kenya." Cambridge: Harvard University.

Glick, Peter, and David E. Sahn. 1997. "Gender and Education Impacts on Employment and Earnings in West Africa: Evidence from Guinea." *Economic Development and Cultural Change* 45 (4): 793–823.

Government of the Federal District of Brazil. 1997. Department of Education (SE), Executive Secretariat for the Bolsa-Escola Program. Cited in Silvio Caccia Bava, "Bolsa-Escola (School Bursary Program): A Public Policy on Minimum Income and Education." IDRC Policy Brief.

Government of Pakistan. 1997. "Pakistan Integrated Household Survey: Round 1 1995–1996." Islamabad. Cited in Oxfam, "Education Report," 2001.

Grossman, Jean Baldwin. 1994. "Evaluating Social Policies: Principles and U.S. Experience." *World Bank Research Observer* 9 (2): 59–180.

Hanushek, Eric. 1995. "Interpreting Recent Research on Schooling in Developing Countries." *World Bank Research Observer* 10 (2): 227–46.

Hanushek, Erik A., and Dennis D. Kimko. 2000. "Schooling, Labor Force Quality, and the Growth of Nations." *American Economic Review* 90 (5): 1184–208.

Haq, M., and K. Haq. 1998. *Human Development in South Asia.* Oxford: Oxford University Press.

Heise, Lori, Mary Elsberg, and Megan Gottemoeller. 1999. "Ending Violence against Women." Population Reports L (11), Population Information Program. Baltimore: Johns Hopkins University School of Public Health.

Heneveld, Ward. 1994. "Planning and Monitoring the Quality of Primary Education in Sub-Saharan Africa." Washington, D.C.: World Bank.

Herz, Barbara. 2002. "Universal Basic Education: What Works." Paper prepared for the Coalition for Basic Education. Washington, D.C.: Academy for Educational Development.

Herz, Barbara, et al. 1991. "Letting Girls Learn: Promising Approaches in Primary and Secondary Education." World Bank Discussion Paper No. 133. Washington, D.C.: World Bank.

Hill, M. Anne, and Elizabeth King. 1995. "Women's Education and Economic Well-Being." *Feminist Economics* 1 (2): 21–46.

Hoddinott, John, and Lawrence Haddad. 1995. "Does Female Income Share Influence Household Expenditures? Evidence from Cote d'Ivoire." *Oxford Bulletin of Economics and Statistics* 57 (1): 77–96.

Hooper, Emma, et al. 1995. "Second Girls' Primary Education Project Final Report: Islamic Republic of Pakistan." Washington, D.C.: Academy for Educational Development.

Ibrahim, Barbara, et al. 2000. "Transitions to Adulthood: A National Survey of Egyptian Adolescents." New York: Population Council.

Inglehart, Ronald, Miguel Basanez, and Alejandro Moreno. 1998. *Human Values and Beliefs: A Cross-Cultural Sourcebook: Political, Religious, Sexual, and Economic Norms in 43 Societies: Findings from the 1990–1993 World Values Survey.* Ann Arbor: University of Michigan Press.

International Labour Organization. 2001. "The Minimum Income for School Attendance Initiative." Geneva: Joint ILO/UNCTAD Advisory Group.

Jamison, Dean, et al. 2001. "The Effect of the AIDS Epidemic on Economic Welfare in Sub-Saharan Africa." Commission on Macroeconomics and Health Working Paper Series No. WG1:13. Geneva: World Health Organization.

Jamison, Dean, and Lawrence J. Lau. 1982. *Farmer Education and Farm Efficiency.* Baltimore: Johns Hopkins University Press.

Jejeebhoy, Shireen J. 1998. "Wife-Beating in Rural India: A Husband's Right? Evidence from Survey Data." *Economic and Political Weekly* 23 (15): 855–62.

———. 1996. *Women's Education, Autonomy, and Reproductive Behavior: Assessing What We Have Learned.* Honolulu: East-West Center.

Jimenez, Emmanual, and Yasuyuki Sawada. 1998. "Do Community-Managed Schools Work? An Evaluation of El Salvador's EDUCO Program." Working Paper Series on Impact Evaluation of Education Reforms Paper No. 8, World Bank Development Research Group. Washington, D.C.: World Bank.

Khandkher, Shahidur. 1998. *Fighting Poverty with Microcredit: Experience in Rural Bangladesh.* Washington, D.C.: World Bank.

———. 1996. "Education Achievements and School Efficiency in Rural Bangladesh." World Bank Discussion Paper No. 319. Washington, D.C.: World Bank.

———. 1988. "Determinants of Women's Time Allocation in Rural Bangladesh." *Economic Development and Cultural Change* 37 (1): 111–26.

Khandkher, S., and Mark Pitt. 2003. "Subsidy to Promote Girls' Secondary Education: The Female Stipend Program in Bangladesh." Washington, D.C.: World Bank.

Kim, Jooseop, Harold Alderman, and Peter Orazem. 1999. "Can Private School Subsidies Increase Enrollment for the Poor? The Quetta Urban Fellowship Program." *World Bank Economic Review* 13 (3): 443–65.

———. 1998. "Can Cultural Barriers Be Overcome in Girls' Schooling? The Community Support Program in Rural Balochistan." Working Paper Series on Impact Evaluation of Education Reforms Paper No. 10, World Bank Development Research Group. Washington, D.C.: World Bank.

King, Elizabeth, et al. 1997. "Colombia's Targeted Education Voucher Program: Features, Coverage, and Participation." Working Paper Series on Impact of Education Reforms Paper No. 3, World Bank Development Research Group. Washington, D.C.: World Bank.

King, Elizabeth, and Rosemary Bellew. 1991. "Gains in the Education of Peruvian Women, 1940–1980." In Barbara Herz and Shahidur Khandkher, eds., "Women's Work, Education, and Family Welfare in Peru." World Bank Discussion Paper No. 116. Washington, D.C.: World Bank.

King, Elizabeth M., and M. Anne Hill, eds. 1993. *Women's Education in Developing Countries.* Baltimore: Johns Hopkins University Press.

King, Elizabeth M., and Lee A. Lillard. 1987. "Education Policy and Schooling Attainment in Malaysia and the Philippines." *Economics of Education Review* 6 (2): 167–81.

King, Elizabeth, and Peter Orazem. 1999. "Evaluating Education Reforms: Four Cases in Developing Countries." *World Bank Economic Review* 13 (3): 409–13.

King, Elizabeth, Peter Orazem, and Elizabeth Paterno. 1999. "Promotion with and without Learning: Effects on Student Dropout." Working Paper Series on Impact Evaluation of Education Reforms Paper No. 18, World Bank Development Research Group. Washington, D.C.: World Bank.

King, Elizabeth M., Peter Orazem, and Darin Wohlgemuth. 1999. "Central Mandates and Local Incentives: The Colombia Education Voucher Program." *World Bank Economic Review* 13 (3): 467–91.

King, Elizabeth, and Berk Ozler. 1998. "What's Decentralization Got to Do with Learning? The Case of Nicaragua's School Autonomy Reform." Working Paper Series on Impact Evaluation of Education Reforms Paper No. 9, World Bank Development Research Group. Washington, D.C.: World Bank.

King, Elizabeth, Berk Ozler, and Laura Rawlings. 1999. "Nicaragua's School Autonomy Reform: Fact or Fiction?" Working Paper Series on Impact Evaluation of Education Reforms Paper No. 19, World Bank Development Research Group. Washington, D.C.: World Bank.

Kingdom, Geeta G. 1998. "Does the Labor Market Explain Lower Female Schooling in India?" *Journal of Development Studies* 35 (1): 39–65.

Kirby, D., et al. 1994. "School-Based Programs to Reduce Risk Behaviors: A Review of Effectiveness." *Public Health Reports* 109 (3): 339–61.

Klasen, Stephan. 1999. "Does Gender Inequality Reduce Growth and Development? Evidence from Cross-Country Regressions." Policy Research Report on Gender and Development Working Paper No. 7. Washington, D.C.: World Bank.

Knox, David M., et al. 1991. *Final Evaluation of the Basic Education Project.* Washington, D.C.: Creative Associates International.

Kremer, Michael. 2003. "Randomized Evaluations of Educational Programs in Developing Countries: Some Lessons." *American Economic Review* 93 (2): 102–15.

———. 1995. "Research on Schooling: What We Know and What We Don't: A Comment on Hanushek." *World Bank Research Observer* 10 (2): 247–54.

Kremer, Michael, Edward Miguel, and Rebecca Thornton. 2003. "Interim Report on a Randomized Evaluation of the Girls' Scholarship Program." Cambridge: Harvard University.

Kremer, Michael, Sylvie Moulin, and Robert Namunyu. 2002. "Unbalanced Decentralization: Results of a Randomized School Supplies Provision Program in Kenya." Cambridge: Harvard University.

Krueger, Alan, and Mikael Lindahl. 2001. "Education for Growth: Why and for Whom?" *Journal of Economic Literature* 39 (4): 1101–36.

Lacey, Mark. 2003. "Primary Schools in Kenya, Fees Abolished, Are Filled to Overflowing." *New York Times.* January 7, A8.

Lassibille, Gerard, Jee-Peng Tan, and Suleiman Sumra. 1998. "Expansion of Private Secondary Education: Experience and Prospects in Tanzania." Working Paper Series on Impact Evaluation of Education Reforms No. 12, World Bank Development Research Group. Washington, D.C.: World Bank.

Lavinas, L. 2001. "The Appeal of Minimum Income Programmes in Latin America." Geneva: International Labour Organization.

Lavy, Victor. 1996. "School Supply Constraints and Children's Educational Outcomes in Rural Ghana." *Journal of Development Economics* 51 (2): 291–314.

Lloyd, C. B., C. E. Kaufman, and P. Hewett. 2000. "The Spread of Primary Schooling in Sub-Saharan Africa: Implications for Fertility Change." *Population and Development Review* 26 (3): 483–515.

Lloyd, C. B., and Barbara Mensch. 1999. "Implication of Formal Schooling for Girls' Transitions to Adulthood in Developing Countries." In Caroline Bledsoe et al., eds., *Critical Perspectives on Schooling and Fertility in the Developing World.* Washington, D.C.: National Academy Press.

Lloyd, Cynthia B., Barbara Mensch, and Wesley Clark. 1998. "The Effects of Primary School Quality on the Educational Participation and Attainment of Kenyan Girls and Boys." Population Council Working Paper 116. New York: Population Council.

Lockheed, Marlaine, and Adriaan Verspoor. 1991. *Improving Primary Education in Developing Countries: A Review of Policy Options.* Oxford: Oxford University Press.

Lokshin, Michael, Elena Glinskaya, and Marito Garcia. 2000. "The Effect of Early Childhood Development Programs on Women's Labor Force Participation and Older Children's Schooling in Kenya." Policy Research Report on Gender and Development Working Paper Series No. 15, World Bank Development Research Group. Washington, D.C.: World Bank.

Malhotra, Anju, Caren Grown, and Rohini Pande. 2003. "Impact of Investments in Female Education on Gender Inequality." Washington, D.C.: International Center for Research on Women.

Mammen, Kristin, and Christina Paxon. 2000. "Women's Work and Economic Development." *Journal of Economic Perspectives* 14 (4): 141–64.

McGinn, Noel, and Allison Borden. 1995. *Framing Questions, Constructing Answers: Linking Research with Education Policy for Developing Countries.* Cambridge: Harvard University Press.

Miguel, Edward, and Michael Kremer. 2004. "Worms: Identifying Impacts on Education and Health in the Presence of Treatment Externalities." *Econometrica* 72 (1): 159–217.

Miller, Judith. 2003. "U.S. Expands Afghan Aid for Maternal and Child Health." Citing a 2002 health survey by UNICEF and the U.S. Centers for Disease Control in Atlanta. *New York Times.* January 27.

Miller-Grandvaux, Yolande, and Karla Yoder. 2002. "A Literature Review of Community Schools in Africa." Washington, D.C.: USAID Bureau for Africa.

Mincer, Jacob. 1974. *Schooling, Experience, and Earnings.* New York: Columbia University Press.

Moock, Peter. 1976. "The Efficiency of Women as Farm Managers: Kenya." *American Journal of Agricultural Economics* 58 (5): 831–35.

Morley, Steven, and David Coady. 2003. *From Social Assistance to Social Development: Targeted Education Subsidies in Developing Countries.* Washington, D.C.: Center for Global Development/International Food Policy Research Institute.

Moseley, Stephen. 2003. "Testimony to the Foreign Operations Subcommittee of the US House of Representatives Committee on Appropriations." May 14.

Ndong-Jatta, Ann Therese. 2002. "Providing Quality Basic Education for All: A New Focus." Presentation by Gambian Secretary of Education. June 11.

Newman, John, Laura Rawlings, and Paul Gertler. 1994. "Using Randomized Control Designs in Evaluating Social Sector Programs in Developing Countries." *World Bank Research Observer* 9 (2): 181–201.

Nilsson, Paula. 2003. "Education for All: Teacher Demand and Supply in Africa." Education International Working Paper No. 12. Brussels: Education International. November.

Obura, A. 1985. "The Image of Girls and Women in Primary Textbooks in Kenya." Nairobi: University of Nairobi.

Odaga, Adhiambo, and Ward Heneveld. 1995. "Girls and Schools in Sub-Saharan Africa: From Analysis to Action." World Bank Technical Paper No. 298. Washington, D.C.: World Bank.

O'Gara, Chloe, et al. 1999. "More, but Not Yet Better: An Evaluation of USAID's Programs and Policies to Improve Girls' Education." USAID Program and Operations Assessment Report No. 25. Washington, D.C.: USAID.

O'Gara, Chloe, and Nancy Kendall. 1996. "Beyond Enrollment: A Handbook for Improving Girls' Experiences in Primary Classrooms." ABEL Project. Washington, D.C.: Creative Associates International.

ORC Macro International Inc. 1995. *Demographic and Health Survey—Kenya.* Calverton, Md.: ORC Macro International Inc.

Organization for Economic Cooperation and Development (OECD). 2004. Donor Aid Charts. Development Co-operation Directorate. Available at http://www.oecd.org/dac/stats.

————. 2003. "Harmonising Donor Practices for Effective Aid Delivery." DAC Guidelines and Reference Series. Paris: OECD.

Over, Mead. 1998. "The Effects of Societal Variables on Urban Rates of HIV Infection in Developing Countries: An Exploratory Analysis." In Martha Ainsworth, Lieve Fransen, and Mead Over, eds., *Confronting AIDS: Evidence from the Developing World.* Brussels and Washington, D.C.: European Commission and World Bank.

Parish, William, and Robert Willis. 1993. "Daughters, Education, and Family Budgets: Taiwan Experiences." *Journal of Human Resources* 28 (4): 863–98.

Population Reference Bureau. 2001. "Abandoning Female Genital Cutting: Prevalence, Attitudes, and Efforts to End the Practice." Washington, D.C.: Population Reference Bureau.

Potter, Michael. 1998. "Microeconomic Foundations of Competitiveness: The Role of Education." Education for All (EFA) paper.

Psacharopoulos, George. 1994. "Returns to Investment in Education: A Global Update." *World Development* 22 (9): 1325–43.

Psacharopoulos, George, and Harry Anthony Patrinos. 2002. "Returns to Investment in Education: A Further Update." World Bank Policy Research Working Paper 2881. Washington, D.C.: World Bank.

————. 2001. "Returns to Investment in Education up to the New Millennium." Washington, D.C.: World Bank.

Puryear, Jeffrey M., ed. 1997. "Partners for Progress, Education and the Private Sector in Latin America and the Caribbean." Washington, D.C.: Inter-American Dialogue.

Quisumbing, Agnes. 1996. "Male-Female Differences in Agricultural Productivity: Methodological Issues and Empirical Evidence." *World Development* 24 (10): 1579–95.

————. 1994. "Improving Women's Agricultural Productivity as Farmers and Workers." Education and Social Policy Department Discussion Paper 37. Washington, D.C.: World Bank.

Rahman, M. Saifur. 2002. "The State of the Economy and the Economic Stabilisation Programme." Speech delivered at Bangladesh Development Forum Meeting, Paris. March 13–15. Available at http://www.gobfinance.org/finance_minister/speech_minister.html.

Reimers, Fernando, and Donald Warwick. 1991. "The Impact of Schools on Achievement in Pakistan." BRIDGES School Effectiveness Studies, Abstract 2. Cambridge: Harvard University.

Ridker, Ronald G., ed. 1997. "Determinants of Educational Achievement and Attainment in Africa: Findings from Nine Case Studies." SD Publication Series, Technical Paper No. 62. Washington, D.C.: USAID.

Rihani, May. 1993. "Strategies for Female Education in the Middle East and North Africa for UNICEF." New York: UNICEF.

Ross, David. 2003. "Results from a Community Randomized Trial in Rural Tanzania: MEMA kwa Vijana Project." Presentation to the Conference on New Findings from Intervention Research: Youth Reproductive Health and Youth HIV Prevention. Washington, D.C. September 9.

Rugh, Andrea. 2000. "Starting Now: Strategies for Helping Girls Complete Primary." SAGE Project. Washington, D.C.: Academy for Educational Development.

Rugh, Andrea, and Heather Bossert. 1998. *Involving Communities: Participation in the Delivery of Education Programs.* Washington, D.C.: Creative Associates International. ABEL Project Consortium. USAID.

Saito, Katrine, Hailu Mekonen, and Daphne Spurling. 1994. "Raising the Productivity of Women Farmers in Sub-Saharan Africa." World Bank Discussion Paper No. 230. Washington, D.C.: World Bank.

Save the Children. 2000. "What's the Difference? The Impact of Early Childhood Development Programs." Kathmandu: Save the Children.

Schultz, T. Paul. Forthcoming. "School Subsidies for the Poor: Evaluating the Mexican PROGRESA Poverty Program." *Journal of Development Economics.*

———. 2002. "Why Governments Should Invest More to Educate Girls." *World Development* 30 (2): 207–25.

———. 1995. *Investment in Women's Human Capital.* Chicago: University of Chicago Press.

———. 1993. "Returns to Women's Schooling." In Elizabeth King and M. Anne Hill, eds., *Women's Education in Developing Countries: Barriers, Benefits, and Policy.* Baltimore: Johns Hopkins University Press.

———. 1992. "Investments in Schooling and Health of Women and Men: Quantities and Returns." Paper prepared for Conference on Women's Human Capital and Development, Bellagio, Italy. May.

———. 1980. "Benefits of Educating Women." World Bank Background Paper Series. Washington, D.C.: World Bank.

Sen, Amartya. 2000. *Development as Freedom.* New York: Anchor Books.

———. 1990a. "Gender and Cooperative Conflict." In Irene Tinker, ed., *Persistent Inequalities: Women and the World.* Oxford: Oxford University Press.

———. 1990b. "More Than 100 Million Women Are Missing." *New York Review of Books* 37 (20) December 20.

———. 1989. "Women's Survival as a Development Problem." *Bulletin of the American Academy of Arts and Sciences* 43 (2): 14–29.

Sen, Purna. 1999. "Enhancing Women's Choices in Responding to Domestic Violence in Calcutta: A Comparison of Employment and Education." *European Journal of Development Research* 11 (2): 65–86.

Sengupta, Somini. 2003. "African Girls' Route to School Still Littered with Obstacles." *New York Times.* December 14, A1.

Shuey, D. A., et al. 1999. "Increased Sexual Abstinence among In-School Adolescents as a Result of School Health Education in Soroti District, Uganda." *Health Education Research* 14 (3): 411–19.

Sipahimanlani, Vandana. 1999. "Education in the Rural Indian Household: The Impact of Household and School Characteristics on Gender Differences." Working Paper 68. New Delhi: National Council of Applied Economic Research.

Smith, Lisa C., and Lawrence Haddad. 1999. "Explaining Child Malnutrition in Developing Countries: A Cross-Country Analysis." International Food Policy Research Institute (IFPRI) Food Consumption and Nutrition Division Discussion Paper 60. Washington, D.C.: IFPRI.

Sperling, Gene. 2003a. "Donor Reactions to the Education for All Initiative." Paper prepared for the UN Millennium Project Task Force on Education and Gender Equality. July.

——— 2003b. "School Is the Front Line against AIDS." *International Herald Tribune.* May 28.

———. 2003c. "Toward a Global Compact on Universal Education." Testimony before the Foreign Operations Subcommittee of the U.S. House of Representatives Committee on Appropriations. May 14.

———. 2002a. "Ethiopia Provides Glimpse of Hope for Its Future." *Bloomberg*. April 15.

———. 2002b. Interview with Ethiopian Education Minister Genet Zewde and PAC Members. Ethiopia. April.

———. 2001. "Toward Universal Education: Making a Promise and Keeping It." *Foreign Affairs* 80 (5): 7–13.

———. 2000. Remarks to the International Consultative Forum on Education for All. Dakar, Senegal. April 28.

Sperling, Gene, and Tom Hart. 2003. "A Better Way to Fight Poverty." *Foreign Affairs* 82 (2): 9–14.

Stasavage, David. Forthcoming. "On the Role of Democracy in Uganda's Move to Universal Primary Education." London School of Economics.

Subbarao, K., and Laura Raney. 1995. "Social Gains from Female Education." *Economic Development and Cultural Change* 44 (1): 105–28.

———. 1993. "Social Gains from Female Education: A Cross-National Study." World Bank Discussion Paper No. 194. Washington, D.C.: World Bank.

Summers, Lawrence H. 1994. "Investing in All the People: Educating Women in Developing Countries." EDI Seminar Paper No. 45. Washington, D.C.: World Bank.

Thomas, Duncan. 1990. "Intra-household Allocation: An Inferential Approach." *Journal of Human Resources* 25 (4): 635–64.

Tietjen, Karen. 2000. "Multisector Support of Basic and Girls' Education." SAGE Project. Washington, D.C.: Academy for Educational Development.

———. 1999. "Community Schools in Mali: A Comparative Cost Study." SD Publication Series Technical Paper No. 97. Washington, D.C.: Health and Human Resources Analysis for Africa Project, USAID.

Tinker, Irene, ed. 1990. *Persistent Inequalities: Women and the World*. Oxford: Oxford University Press.

Tomasevski, Katarina. 2003. *Education Denied: Costs and Remedies*. New York: Zed Books.

UNAIDS. 2003. "HIV/AIDS Epidemic Update 2003." New York: UNAIDS. December.

———. 2000. *The UNAIDS Report on Global HIV/AIDS Epidemic*. Geneva: UNAIDS. Available at http://www.unaids.org/publications/documents.

———. 1999. *The UNAIDS Report*. Geneva: UNAIDS. Available at http://www.unaids.org/publications/documents/responses/theme/repjuly99.doc.

UNDP. 2003. *Arab Human Development Report 2003*. New York: UNDP.

———. 2001. *Human Development Report 2001*. Oxford: Oxford University Press.

UNESCO. 2003a. *Education for All Global Monitoring Report 2003/4*. Paris: UNESCO.

———. 2003b. *Regional Report on South and East Asia*. Paris: UNESCO Institute for Statistics.

———. 2002a. *EFA Global Monitoring Report: Is the World on Track?* Paris: UNESCO.

———. 2002b. *Gender, Education, and HIV/AIDS*. Instituto Promundo. Rio de Janeiro: UNESCO.

———. 2002c. "Press Release for *A Strategic Approach: HIV/AIDS and Education*." Available at http://portal.unesco.org/ev.php?URL.

———. 2000. "Women and Girls: Education, Not Discrimination." Paris: UNESCO.

UNICEF. 2003. *State of the World's Children 2004.* New York: UNICEF.

———. 2002a. "Case Studies on Girls' Education." New York: UNICEF.

———. 2002b. "Education and HIV Prevention." Citing data from Kenya Demographic and Health Survey. New York: UNICEF.

———. 2001. *Fourth Consolidated Report to the Government of Norway on the UNICEF African Girls' Education Initiative.* New York: UNICEF Program Division/Education Section.

———. 2000. "Absorbing Social Shocks, Protecting Children and Reducing Poverty." New York: UNICEF.

———. 1999. *The State of the World's Children, 2000.* Oxford: Oxford University Press.

UN Population Division. 2003. *Population, Education, and Development: The Concise Report.* Department of Economic and Social Affairs. New York: UN.

U.S. Agency for International Development. 1998. *A New Focus on Girls' and Women's Education: Successful USAID Education Investment Strategies.* Report in Brief. WID Works, USAID Office of Women in Development. Washington, D.C.: USAID.

U.S. Foreign Agriculture Service. 2003. *The Global Food for Education Pilot Program: A Review of Project Implementation and Impact.* Report to the U.S. Congress. February.

Vandemoortele, J., and E. Delamonica. 2000. "Education 'Vaccine' against HIV/AIDS." *Current Issues in Comparative Education* 3 (1). Available at http://www.tc.columbia.edu/cice/articles/jved131.htm.

Vermeersch, Christel. 2002. "School Meals, Educational Achievement, and School Competition: Evidence from a Randomized Experiment." Cambridge: Harvard University.

Warwick, Donald, and Fernando Reimers. 1995. *Hope or Despair? Learning in Pakistan's Primary Schools.* Westport: Praeger.

———. 1991a. "Good Schools and Poor Schools in Pakistan: How They Differ." BRIDGES School Effectiveness Studies, Abstract 1. Harvard Institute for Development Studies. Cambridge: Harvard University.

———. 1991b. "Who Completes Primary School in Pakistan?" BRIDGES School Effectiveness Studies, Abstract 3. Harvard Institute for Development Studies. Cambridge: Harvard University.

Warwick, Donald, Fernando Reimers, and Noel McGinn. 1989a. "The Implementation of Educational Innovations in Primary Education in Pakistan." BRIDGES papers on Primary Education in Pakistan, Report No. 1. Harvard Institute for Development Studies. Cambridge: Harvard University.

———. 1989b. "Teacher Characteristics and Student Achievement in Math and Science." BRIDGES papers on Primary Education in Pakistan, Report No. 5. Harvard Institute for Development Studies. Cambridge: Harvard University.

Wax, Emily. 2003. "For Kenyans, Time to Change Is Now; In Rejecting Legacy of Moi's Corruption, People Outpace Reform-Minded Leaders." *Washington Post.* February 3, A18.

World Bank. 2004. "Education for All Fast Track Initiative Progress Report." April 25. Washington, D.C.: World Bank.

———. 2003. *Development Indicators 2004.* Washington, D.C.: World Bank.

———. 2002a. "Achieving Universal Education for All by 2015: Simulation Results for 47 Low-Income Countries." Human Development Network, Africa Region. Washington, D.C.: World Bank.

———. 2002b. "Education and HIV/AIDS: A Window of Hope." World Bank Education Section, Human Development Department. Washington D.C.: World Bank.

———. 2002c. "Education for Dynamic Economies: Action Plan to Accelerate Progress towards Education for All (EFA)." Washington, D.C.: World Bank.

———. 2001a. *Engendering Development.* World Bank Policy Research Report. Washington, D.C., and Oxford: World Bank and Oxford University Press.

———. 2001b. "Pioneering Support for Girls' Secondary Education: The Bangladesh Female Secondary School Assistance Project." Washington, D.C.: World Bank.

———. 2000a. *Development Indicators 2000.* Washington, D.C.: World Bank.

———. 2000b. "Education for All: From Jomtien to Dakar and Beyond." Paper Prepared for the World Education Forum in Dakar, Senegal. April 28.

———. 1999. "Education Sector Strategy." Washington, D.C.: World Bank.

———. 1997a. "Pakistan: New Approaches to Education: The Northern Areas Community School Program." Washington, D.C.: World Bank.

———. 1997b. *Pakistan: Toward a Strategy for Elementary Education.* Report 16670-PAK. Washington, D.C.: World Bank.

———. 1996a. "Improving Basic Education in Pakistan." Report 14960-PAK. Washington, D.C.: World Bank.

———. 1996b. "Niger Poverty Assessment: A Resilient People in a Harsh Environment." Washington, D.C.: World Bank. Cited in Oxfam, "Education Report," 2001.

———. 1990. "Gender and Poverty in India." Washington, D.C.: World Bank.

World Food Programme. 2001. "School Feeding Works for Girls' Education." WFP Report. Rome: World Food Programme.

World Health Organization. 1998. "Female Genital Mutilation." Geneva: World Health Organization.

About the Authors

Barbara Herz, a member of the Council on Foreign Relations, has worked on and written about girls' education for more than 20 years. In the 1970s she headed the U.S. Agency for International Development division responsible for policy in education, health, and population. She was a member of the U.S. delegation to the UN Conference for Women in Copenhagen in 1980. She then worked from 1981–99 at the World Bank, where she launched the Women in Development division and then headed another division covering education, health, and population in Bangladesh, Pakistan, and Sri Lanka. She was a member of the World Bank Delegation to the UN Conference for Women in Nairobi in 1986. She later served as senior adviser for social sectors to Treasury Secretary Lawrence Summers and is now an economic consultant living in Jackson Hole, Wyoming. She holds a BA from Wellesley and a PhD from Yale.

Gene B. Sperling is the director of the Center for Universal Education at the Council on Foreign Relations. Mr. Sperling previously served as national economic adviser to President Clinton from 1996–2000, and represented the Clinton administration at the 2000 UN World Education Forum in Dakar, Senegal, where he delivered one of the keynote addresses. Mr. Sperling is a member of the UN Millennium Task Force on Gender Equality and Education, and served on the Education Expert Group of the World Economic Forum's Global Governance Initiative. Mr. Sperling also serves as U.S. chair of the Global Campaign for Education. He graduated from Yale Law School and holds a BA from the University of Minnesota.